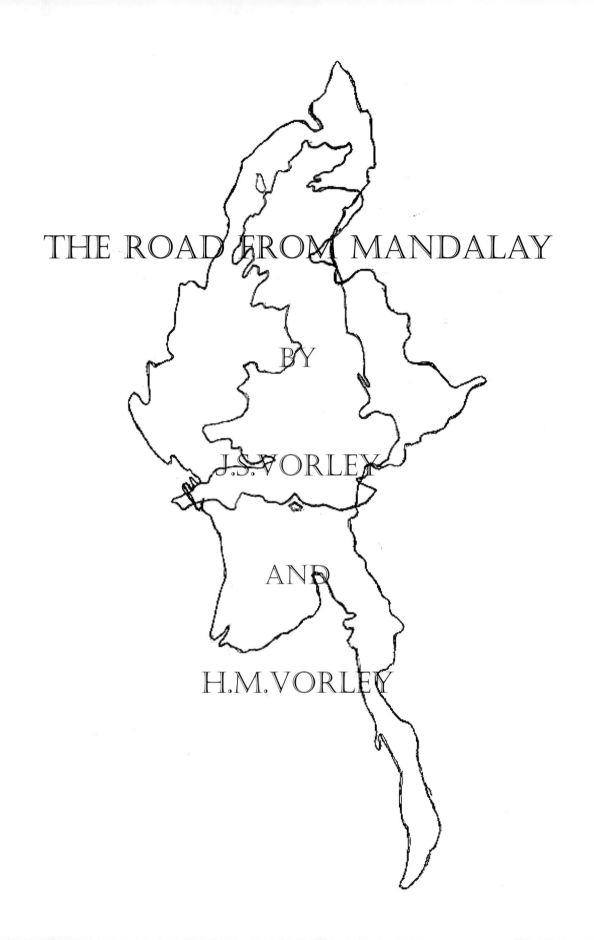

THE ROAD FROM MANDALAY

BY

J.S.VORLEY

AND

H.M.VORLEY

THE ROAD FROM MANDALAY

BY

J. S. AND H. M. VORLEY

First Published in Great Britain 2002
by
WILTON 65
HERNES KEEP, WINKFIELD, WINDSOR. SL4 4SY.

Paperback ISBN 0 947828 97 4
Caseback ISBN 0 947828 92 3

The author and his wife in Rangoon in 1941

INTRODUCTION

By

COLONEL THE RIGHT HONOURABLE SIR REGINALD DORMAN-SMITH, P.C., G.B.E.
GOVERNOR OF BURMA 1941-46

To be at the receiving end of a successful invasion by a ruthless enemy is an experience which fortunately few of us British have had to undergo. It is a grim experience, which we thought might come our way after Dunkirk.

It so happened that at that time it was my privilege, as a military member of the Home Defence Executive, to be closely connected with the feverish work of preparing this country to resist invasion. The Home Defence Executive was the link between General Headquarters (Home Forces) and the civilian Departments of Government. In order to test our anti-invasion preparations the Commander-in-Chief Home Forces laid on realistic exercises, my part in which convinced me that if Hitler were to make a landing in strength we should be in for a very rough time. During these paper exercises we had our moments of chaos. Refugees cluttered the roads; communications broke down so that it was impossible for the 'centre' to get a clear picture of what was happening; rumours and still more rumours abounded; the over-running of gaols and lunatic asylums created its own problem; sabotage and 5th column activities added to our (paper) troubles.

But after these exercises I was always able to go back to White's and relax, little thinking that it would ever be my fate to hold a position of rare responsibility in a country which was to be overwhelmed by an invasion.

Here in our British Isles invasion would have been bad enough but at least the battle would have been fought on our own soil and we would have been among our own people. In Burma it was different. The vast majority of the Burman people had but little idea of what the war was about anyway; instead of dealing with a united homogenous country, we had to cope with Burmans, British, Anglos, Indians of all sorts and descriptions, Chinese, together with oddments of many other nations. There was no common language and no common code of behaviour or diet, such as there would have been here.

In Great Britain we prepared for an invasion which never took place; in Burma we had to meet an invasion for which we were pathetically unprepared.

In an emergency individuals count much more than paper organizations. The lesson I had learned in London was that if a 'soldier's battle' had to be fought one must get hold of the right 'soldier'.

Vorley's own peculiar personal qualities marked him out as an almost automatic choice for the most difficult of all jobs with which civilians have to deal during an invasion – the care of refugees. These qualities can be recognized from his own words in the pages which follow. He was impetuous, intolerant at times and always determined to get his own way, a first-class cutter of red-tape, quite fearless but above all a man of great human sympathy, which is what counts most when you are dealing with refugees.

He now tells his story, assisted, as always, by his wife. What we owed in Burma to those women who stuck it out should never be forgotten. The Vorleys tell their story in their own way. I and others might like to argue with them and ask them to accept it as a fact that their frustrations were our frustrations though perhaps on a different 'level'. But this is their story in which they set out to tell us just what they did and just what they thought when events were right on top of them. Theirs is a story of what the man and the woman on the spot were doing on their own under incredibly difficult circumstances.

It is a story of brave endeavour, of sheer guts and of great achievement. It is also a tragic story. But though there may have been anything up to ten thousand casualties on the way out from Burma to the comparative safety of India, Vorley and his devoted staff enabled more than four hundred thousand refugees to reach that safety within a span of a few short weeks.

We all mourn the loss of those who died on the way out but we also salute those grand people, both working from within Burma and those toiling from Assam to meet us with out-stretched hands, who enabled almost half a million souls to survive. This is an achievement of which Vorley has every reason to be proud.

FOREWORD

LIEUTENANT GENERAL SIR THOMAS JACOMB HUTTON, K.C.I.E., C.B., M.C.

It is, perhaps, too early to arrive at a balanced view of events during the Japanese invasion of Burma. So far the story has been distorted by too many unbalanced and highly imaginative accounts and by the rumours and recriminations with which the time abounded. It is a relief, therefore, to turn to a realistic account of one of the most tragic and heroic aspects of that campaign.

Mr. Vorley would, I think, be the first to admit that there may be another side to the story, though he does not shrink from criticism of authority, or of individuals, when he feels it is due. He has been kind enough to correct various errors of fact which I have pointed out to him and I will not attempt here to deal with criticisms of the actions of the military authorities. He describes the situation as it appeared to him at the time and it is inevitable that in such conditions there should be inaccurate information and unfounded criticism. The same was also true on the military side in regard to the actions of the civilians and the civil administration.

There were many failures in Burma, military and civilian, British, Burmese and Indian. It is, however, a relief to recall that at the top there was none of that friction and mutual criticism between the military and civilians that is so often a feature of an unsuccessful campaign. The Burma Government, and not least the Burmese Ministers, did everything they could to support the military effort though naturally we did not always agree as to the best way of doing it. We on our part tried to turn a sympathetic ear to the difficulties of the civil government and the population. The failure of some of the troops, many of them half trained and unprepared for war, was more than redeemed by the heroism of others. The virtual collapse of some of the administrative and public services was balanced by the initiative, energy and endurance of others, amongst which the Vorleys and their helpers must take a high place.

The British women, with few exceptions, were beyond praise and a special tribute must be paid to the Anglo-Burmans, Anglo-Indians and Karens who played such a noble part. The patient Indian refugee deserves our sympathy and our admiration, he only needed leadership and to be told what to do. Even the much-abused Burman was not half as bad as he was painted by some people at the time. Many soldiers and refugees owed their safety to the kindly action of Burmese villagers, some of whom took considerable risks to protect them. A special word of praise must also be given to the British planters in Assam who set a magnificent example of well-organized voluntary effort.

The military can, I think, claim that by the timely evacuation of civilians from Rangoon they saved them from the horrors of massacre or a Japanese prison camp, action for which they were much criticized at the time. It was only after considerable pressure on the sea transport authorities that military transports were made available to refugees but they must have saved many thousands of lives. The decision not to carry out a scorched earth policy and to leave local small craft and rice mills intact did much to mitigate the horrors of war for the civil population. Even the decision, made on military grounds, to hold up for a time the passage of refugees over the Burma road enabled the route to be considerably improved and stocks of rice to be established.

Mr. Vorley is, I feel, a little hard on those responsible for civil defence; he had, perhaps, an impossible task, too little time and too few reliable personnel to set up an organization fit to stand the test of war.

The worst tragedy, perhaps, was on the Prome road and it is difficult not to feel that more might have been done to mitigate it. The partial failure to utilize to the best advantage the resources available for the evacuation of wounded, and civilian refugees, by air must be laid at the door of the authorities in India, so much more might have been done. I am glad, however, that I was able, by my personal intervention, to do something to speed it up.

It is interesting, when reading this account of one aspect of the war in Burma, to consider what might have happened in India under similar circumstances. Had Calcutta and other Indian towns been bombed with the same intensity as Rangoon, and had the Japanese invaded the thickly populated areas of India, could the situation have been kept under control even to the extent it was in Burma? If the Burma campaign did nothing else it imposed five months' delay on the Japanese and may thus have been instrumental in averting an invasion of India and all the horrors that would have accompanied it.

PREFACE

This is the history of the evacuation of Burma in 1941-42. It is not a literary masterpiece embellished with imaginary conversations and highly-coloured descriptions of courage and cowardice; there are no trimmings to make it sensational; it is a true narrative of events as they happened and were dealt with by a very loyal, hardworking band of men and women who, serving under me, formed the Department of Civil Evacuation of the Government of Burma.

On several occasions my wife and I were separated and she has therefore included her experiences in separate chapters.

Many of those who were in Burma during that period have criticized my action in keeping on my staff my wife and the other ladies after Rangoon fell; on one occasion in Katha they were told by an officer that they were a damned nuisance. I have been accused of heartless cruelty in exposing them to the danger of capture, possibly torture or worse by the Japanese and to the risk and hardship of the trek out to India, but I remain unconverted.

Those critics were, I fear, thinking mainly of themselves and of the possible extra responsibility and trouble they might experience in having to look after these women. I am sure those ladies thought with me of the tens of thousands of women and children who in those days were utterly dependent on the help, courage and confidence we could give them, support which could only be given with real understanding and sympathy by their own sex. But most of us, I think, both men and women, felt it was our duty. Burma was a part of the Empire and we in that country were there for a purpose, to set an example, to bring into the lives of the people justice and peace, to give them confidence, to teach them to be self-reliant and to look on us as their guardian and friend. Peace and security vanished with the arrival of the Japanese; the people had not yet attained self-reliance and to leave them to fend for themselves at such a time would have been a repudiation of all the principles on which we have based our administration in the Empire. That duty is equally applicable to women as it is to men in whatever part of the Commonwealth of Nations they may be.

The girls and the collection of men from all walks of life who formed my staff set an example of loyalty, unremitting toil and self-sacrifice which I shall never forget and probably never again experience. I was a stranger to almost all of them when they joined, few of them knew what they had let themselves in for, few of them knew if they would ever escape out of Burma after Rangoon fell, yet not once during those six hectic months did I hear a word of criticism or of protest at the hours or nature of the work, and there was hardly a single case of slackness or neglect of duty. They put their whole heart and soul into everything they did and, though often tired out, often depressed and often hungry, they maintained an air of cheerfulness and camaraderie which created that atmosphere of self-confidence without which we could never have coped with the many trials and worries.

To those loyal and grand men and women I dedicate this book, and I know I speak for all of them when I add my heartfelt thanks to my wife. Her constant presence, never excitable, her quiet efficient ability to cope with her multifarious jobs and her understanding and interest in the welfare of every member of the staff, did so much to keep up our morale and produce such an excellent and happy team.

J.S.V.
Totland Bay, August 1950

SUPPLEMENT BY KENNETH VORLEY

As Jack and Helen Vorley's only child, I am glad that at long last it has been possible to publish this record of their incredible achievements. This has been largely due to the encouragement and advice given to me by Lord and Lady Holderness.

Contrary to general opinion those who worked in tropical climates had difficulties to contend with even in peacetime, the problem of bringing up children being one of them. After being born in the U.K. I was taken to Burma with my parents at six months old, but I had to be shipped off to my grandmother in Calcutta for the jungle touring season;and came home for good when I was almost seven years old. The result was that when in 1964 (aged 37) I and my family were having Christmas with my mother, she pointed out that it was only the fifth time she had shared Christmas with me since I was born!

I was fortunate in my last two years in Burma to be allowed to accompany my parents on their jungle tours. As moving the tented camp every so often could involve a 12 mile trek, my 'transport' was a white pony called Mary Rose led by an Indian servant. Wild life was more abundant in those days so the pug marks of tiger and leopard were occasionally seen round the tents, while I delighted in watching the elephants - used for carrying all the gear - being washed in the local stream. My unusual life led to a misunderstanding when I was sent to boarding school in the U.K. After a month there the joint headmistresses wrote to my parents to say that I was settling down well but, unfortunately, they had to report that I was an inveterate liar! I had been regaling my friends with nonsense stories about living in the jungle and riding on elephants - all of which my parents had to confirm was exactly the life I had been leading with them.

As the Fourteenth Army and anything to do with Burma was almost a forgotten theatre of war in 1941-1945, I hope this heart-warming story provides an essential patch to help make the wider tapestry of those events more complete.

[As the Indian sub-continent had not been divided into the independent states of India, Pakistan and Bangladesh at the time covered by this book, the term 'Indian' in this book refers to all members from the three countries of the sub-continent.]

My wife with Kenneth on Mary Rose, 1931

CHAPTER I

By the end of May 1940 we had packed up our luggage in Toungoo in Lower Burma and my wife and I were looking forward eagerly to catching a boat for England. The war news from the west was far from hopeful, but we had not been home since 1936 and our young son in England was due to enter a public school. Owing to my wife's illness in 1932, necessitating her return to England with the boy, I had only seen him for about four out of the thirteen years since he had been born.

I had been in the 'Army in Burma Reserve of Officers' since 1923, but the military authorities considered that at the age of forty-two I was no longer young enough for active service and, with many other Reserve Officers, I had been asked to resign. My normal duties as a Forest Officer were not particularly arduous and as it hardly gave one the satisfaction of making any serious contribution to the war effort, I felt that by getting home I might find some more useful employment.

Then 1st June arrived and Dunkirk, with the cancellation of the sailing of our boat and of most other passenger boats. We spent a day in Rangoon visiting all shipping offices and were finally offered passages on a Bibby boat. The offer, however, included the warning that the previous boat had been commandeered at Colombo where all passengers had been, and still were, stranded. Little hope was held out that this later boat would be more fortunate. The only alternative was a boat to San Francisco and then by train to New York at a cost of about £160 each, and then no guarantee of a boat from New York to the United Kingdom.

We decided to take our leave locally and spent a very delightful three months motoring round the Shan States. At the expiration of my leave, I was posted to special duty with Headquarters in Rangoon.

Though in the west the war was at such a critical stage, life in Rangoon seemed to have changed little. A few well-known faces had disappeared, but weekly races at the Turf Club and Sailing Club, dances at the Gymkhana and Boat Clubs, and paper chases at the Country Club continued with their peace time regularity. Except for a slight reduction in supplies of whiskey, the war seemed to have brought little hardship.

Contrary to the general impression Europeans in the East worked hard, but they also played hard. Commercial offices started at 8 a.m., sometimes earlier, and except for a short break for lunch the younger officers would carry on till 6 p.m., often later. Government office hours were from 10.a.m. to 5 p.m. without a break, but it was seldom any officer went home for tea without a full basket full of files which would keep him busy for two or three hours that evening or early the next morning. If there were any outdoor inspections to carry out they were done in the cool of the early morning.

In the evenings one would usually go for a sail on the Lakes or there would be golf at Mingaladon, tennis at the Gymkhana, rowing at the Boat Club or swimming at Kokine. On Saturdays there was always the Gymkhana Club dance from where the bright young things migrated to the Silver Grill Night Club. On Sundays, after a morning's strenuous exercise, one usually had sufficient beer and curry to ensure a peaceful afternoon's sleep. Almost everyone went to the cinema in the evening, then dinner and bed. It was a grand life and Rangoon, in spite of the very humid atmosphere, could be most enjoyable.

When we arrived there in October 1940 a Civil Defence Department had been formed and officials and business men had volunteered for service in different branches, but only a very few seemed to take their duties seriously. After all, the war was thousands of miles away and the possibility of any part of the British Empire being attacked, much less captured, was unthinkable. To express such views branded one almost as a fifth columnist.

I was on tour in the forest from November 1940 till May 1941, and on my return to Rangoon spent occasional evenings as a volunteer at the Headquarters of the Civil Evacuation Branch until the following November, when I left for a preliminary inspection of the accessible forests on the eastern slopes of the Pegu Yomas. I had planned a long forest tour from December to March, had selected a site for a Christmas camp and left my wife to collect acceptances from a dozen or so friends who would join us for Christmas week.

We still dream about those Christmas camps when, in the evenings, we sat round an enormous fire of logs dragged in and piled six or seven feet high by my elephants. We would look on to a stream which had been dammed up by the villagers to form a perfect swimming pool, and around us would be the dense forest with the ever constant chorus of jungle noises. Christmas dinner would include roast peacock or peafowl, possibly a turkey as well, often a succulent well-hung joint of wild pig, followed by a plum pudding blazing in brandy. Each morning we would be out for a jungle fowl shoot, returning to pints of stream-cooled beer followed by a cold buffet, then out again in the evening for another shoot.

On the 30th November I left my five baggage elephants and my tents just outside Pegu and came into Rangoon to collect my wife and stores for the long tour. On arrival at the capital I heard that Government had fixed 'black out' exercises from 1st December to the 7th, the first full-scale practice the Civil Defence Department had experienced, and I found myself on duty at Evacuation Headquarters necessitating a postponement – I hoped temporary – of my tour programme.

It appeared that many changes had taken place in the previous month or so due to the ideas brought out from England by a Civil Defence expert appointed by the Burma Government. Unfortunately he did not, and would not, realise that the actions behaviour and loyalty of the people in England could not serve as any criterion for the attitude of the population of a Far Eastern country. In Burma there were over a million Indians and Chinese who had no roots in the country, and who, particularly the Indians, were as apprehensive of the natural inhabitants, the Burmese, as they were of any invading force.

This large population of Indians needs some explanation. The Burman has never been partial to manual labour, and, like all but the 'Untouchables' or sweeper class of Indians, he has always refused to work on conservancy labour. This manual work had to be carried out by the Indian who, therefore, in Burma occupied a very vital position in the economic life of the country, and particularly in Rangoon. There the port, the railway and goods yards, the Corporation, the large rice and timber mills, the oil refinery and most of the factories depended almost entirely on Indian labour.

After the Indian Mutiny and the conquest of Burma several vast areas were set aside in the country for cultivation by Indians, such areas then being dense virgin forest. These settlers had since multiplied considerably.

Most of the Indians, particularly the labour force, were of the poorest class from south India, accustomed and willing to live on the cheapest and often the least nutritious of diets. They were good workers and could work hard, but had not the stamina for sustained effort. They had no permanent

A Forest Department 'dak' bungalow

The author and his wife with elephants for the camping equipment

interest in the country and would send most of their weekly wages back to India, to which country they periodically returned.

Amongst the better class Indians there was a large number of moneylenders, all of whom had agents in almost every village up country. Since the slump of 1932 these men had been particularly rapacious, and by foreclosure, had acquired ownership of enormous areas of paddy land. Loan transactions were most complicated. The interest fixed, usually at exorbitant rates, would be repaid in baskets of paddy, but would be demanded when the paddy price was high, which would increase the rate very considerably. For example: supposing the rate was 20 per cent and that would be very low, the interest due might be fixed at ten baskets of paddy, the price then standing at 85 rupees per hundred baskets. Payment of interest would, however, be demanded, i.e. ten baskets, when the price was 110 rupees per hundred baskets. The cultivator might have had a bad crop and could not pay, so he would get another loan to pay off the interest due, and so it would go on year after year, the improvident and uneducated Burmese cultivator not having the faintest idea what he owed until suddenly his land was acquired.

In the years immediately preceding the Japanese war, the more nationalistic Burmese politicians and political parties had started a crusade against the Indian, and had passed very strict immigration laws to apply to these non-indigenous workers. There was, therefore, every reason for the Indian in Burma to feel insecure should British protection disappear.

By December 1941 a belated start had been made in Civil Defence. Shelters and water tanks had been constructed and wardens had been recruited and were under training, but an excellent scheme was cancelled which had provided for the evacuation from Rangoon of all the population who were not absolutely essential to carry on the war effort in the event of the town being bombed and possibly attacked.

The population were now expected to behave like those who had stood up to the Battle of Britain; there was to be no evacuation except of the priority classes, such as the deaf and dumb institutions, the aged and sick, some, not all, of the schools and some, again not all, of the hospitals.

The officer and his deputy originally responsible for the Evacuation scheme had been transferred to other duties and with them had gone many of the original records and details of the organization. I found myself for hours on end during this 'black out' exercise sitting at Evacuation Headquarters with nothing to do and not knowing, and being unable to find out, what anyone else was doing or was supposed to be doing. The Evacuation scheme had been cancelled, almost in its entirety; then why have an Evacuation staff? That was the attitude, and no one responsible in the Civil Defence organisation took the slightest interest in us sitting wasting our time in this requisitioned Girls High School, which proudly displayed in large letters on a notice board outside 'Evacuation Headquarters'.

I thought of my five elephants waiting at Pegu, the lovely camp sites under the shade of enormous bamboo clumps, many of these sites already cleared and waiting for my tents. I had visions of the hundreds of jungle fowl which, after the reaping of paddy, were only waiting for beaters and guns to provide such a succulent addition to the camp menu, and I decided I was wasting my time in Rangoon so applied to be allowed to return to the Forest Department. 'Applied' is rather too polite a term to express what actually happened. I was so annoyed and utterly disgusted with my treatment during the past few days that my interview that evening with the Civil Defence expert was decidedly acrimonious on both sides. When I left I was quite convinced he would be only too pleased to see the last of me for ever, and it was, therefore, with very mixed feelings that I answered the telephone in my house next morning, to be told by this gentleman that I had been appointed Director of Civil Evacuation, Rangoon. From that hour he gave me his full support and never by any sign showed that he remembered my wrathful and candid criticisms at that interview.

That morning I visited various authorities to find out what my duties and responsibilities would be, and came to the sorrowful conclusion that my Christmas camp would have to be merely a wishful thought.

Little could be accomplished during the remainder of the exercise, as without a list of the original volunteer staff, they could not be contacted and I did not know to what duties they had been posted under the original scheme should an exercise of this nature occur. I well remember going out in the middle of the night to a pitch dark main railway station and at the top of my voice enquiring if there were any Evacuation staff on duty. The same action was taken at the docks and the river boat jetties, repeatedly so, as the staff were on four-hour shifts. Lorries had been detailed to collect each shift from their houses throughout the city, but would return empty or with only one or two women. There were supposed to be recognised collecting points, but either the drivers had no knowledge of them or the staff lost their way in the dark. To use a cockney expression, it was a real good 'muck up' each night which all had to be sorted out the next morning. Those few remaining days were not, therefore, wasted and we almost welcomed Government's orders that the exercise should be continued for another week.

The next morning 8th December, I got another telephone call at my house as I was getting dressed. This was the news that the Japanese had declared war, also instructions to take immediate steps to evacuate the priority classes. That was on a Monday morning; I went to the office, having my breakfast sent down there, and did not get back to my house again till about midnight on the following Thursday, by which time we had the organisation back to almost its original strength.

Those four days and nights seemed as hectic as it could possibly be, but the difficulties and confusion and never-ending worries, largely due to my lack of knowledge of previous arrangements, proved to be merely a kindergarten training for the unbelievable and incredible tasks that were to come our way during the next six months.

One of the most immediate tasks to tackle was a racket in connection with the feeding of the permanent staff of three evacuation camps which had been retained when the original plan had been cancelled. This permanent staff included a detachment of about fifty ladies who had volunteered at the Race Course camp. I discovered that contracts had been placed with catering firms at prices which were staggering; the cost per head was more than my wife was spending to feed both of us. As soon as I cancelled the contracts and arranged for the staff to feed themselves there were storms of protest from the caterers who, I then discovered, had been paying in advance a very appreciable commission to a Burmese member of the staff who had executed the contracts. He soon went.

A far more difficult job was the volunteer women's unit. I admired them for volunteering, but their main task if mass evacuation of the Indian population ever did occur would be in the care of the women and children, and many of those ladies were hardly suited to the dirt and rough and tumble such work would entail. A few of the younger ones I should have liked to keep, but many were mothers of children and, if there was going to be heavy bombing, they themselves would have to leave, as many of them did after the second raid. Every day these ladies arrived at the camp, brought out their knitting or sewing and had a good old gossip, and then polished off an excellent meal at the expense of the Evacuation

Department before returning home; and there was not a single male or female evacuee in the camp. I finally dispensed with their services but the repercussions lasted for days, including a request for an explanation from His Excellency the Governor. I wonder why it is that ladies can be so very delightful and charming individually and so extremely difficult en masse?

The priority classes comprised institutions which either for financial reasons depended for their existence mainly on the generosity of the Rangoon public, or those for whom Rangoon had no essential ties.

Amongst the first class were the Roman Catholic charitable concerns, and for them alternative accommodation had to be found in the suburbs, but away from probable targets such as docks, railway stations, power stations etc.

The wonderful courage and self-sacrifice, and with it all cheerfulness and sense of humour of the sisters, nuns and priests with these charitable Institutions was an inspiration. It would be impossible to forget the Mother Superior and staff of the Home for the Aged, which had to be moved three times as each successive building was taken over by the military. Most of this staff had been through Communist riots in China, and had described to me the anxious days and nights they had spent sheltering under tables with bullets and shells piercing windows and walls; yet now they were very loath to leave their original home in the centre of the target area in Rangoon, and protested most strongly at finally being moved out of the town. When I met them shortly after Rangoon had been retaken by the XIV Army in 1945, after four years of Japanese occupation, the Mother Superior was on her death bed, one or two sisters and several of the inmates had died, but they had got back to their original Home. Those that were left were still cheerful, and I can see now the twinkle in their eyes when in shocked tones they begged me to send them cloth as they had no knickers left.

Another very gallant band of sisters and nuns controlled several orphanages and homes, which included the care of over fifty women of all ages rescued from the oldest profession in the world. Here again I met the twinkle when I was told how one of those naughty old ladies - and this particular one was over sixty - had sat up in bed one morning and remarked: "When this b----y war is over I shall have my hair dyed red." I had never realised before that Roman Catholic sisters could be so very human.

Those old ladies were evacuated, also part of the orphanages, to Insein outside Rangoon, and shortly afterwards the buildings got direct hits in a bombing raid and were burnt to the ground.

Houses for the deaf and dumb and for the incurables and various other orphanages and schools were moved either by river boat or by train, and we were lucky in having a fortnight unmolested by Japanese bombers to complete this work and to complete the reorganization of the Department.

Some of that evacuation will forever be stamped on my memory. Walking down a platform at the main railway station with both hands held very tight by little blind children, a child on either side, all of them so cheerful and so thrilled and interested in what was to them almost a very special treat, and I could only wonder what was going to happen to all of them. On another occasion the incurables were taken from their Home by ambulances down to the river jetty to be embarked on a steamer for Mandalay. All of them, old men and women who had for years rested happily in the loving care of the Roman Catholic nuns, now had to undergo this upheaval, they and I little realizing that in four month's time they would be left in Mandalay at the mercy of the Japanese.

It was a queer period as with the evacuation of the priority classes our job was officially over, yet no one accepted that fact; staff was collected - all volunteers - and plans laid, mainly in accordance with the original scheme for some sort of eventuality, though what that might be no one could tell. The Civil Defence Chief left me alone; he paid me a visit one night and was most impressed when one of my girls ushered him into my private sanctum, where I had an easy chair, and produced a whiskey and soda and ice.

All the staff being volunteers, there was little expenditure incurred by the Department and I could make my plans and arrangements with officialdom being very little the wiser. By Christmas Day we were almost ready to put into operation a good deal of the original scheme which had been cancelled.

The staff in the main were school teachers from Government, Government-aided, and private schools. Those from Government or Government-aided schools were mostly Anglo-Indians or Anglo-Burmans. The majority of teachers in private schools were Indians or Chinese. The very few officers on the staff were Government officials with a sprinkling of European businessmen. The Christmas holidays had started at many schools enabling the teachers on my staff to adhere to a definite roster, but I could see confusion when the schools reopened.

Government officials as volunteers were not very satisfactory, as they could seldom follow a hard and fast roster and frequently had to be relieved of their duties. Under the original scheme all non-essential Government offices were to be moved up country; this had been officially cancelled but several Head of Departments which were not vital to the war effort in Rangoon were toying with the idea of moving out of the town, which if put into effect might deprive me of many officers.

The lack of a Deputy to take my place should the occasion occur was another headache. There were daily conferences here, conferences there, visits and arrangements to be made with the Head of each Institution or Home to be evacuated, yet all day my telephone would be ringing. More often than not to start with the conversations would be on trivial matters; individuals or Heads of Department not knowing the scheme had been cancelled asking what they should do, enquiring when I would complete arrangements for their evacuation. Had I arranged accommodation for them up country, would I let them have six lorries for their files and records – I had not a single vehicle of any sort - did I think it safe for Mr. So-and-So to keep his wife and children in Rangoon; one perturbed gentleman kept me for about a quarter of an hour trying to find out if I thought his wife should have her imminent baby in Rangoon or should be moved at once to India. If I was out they would go on ringing, and often getting back to the office at 7 or 8 p.m. I would find a pile of messages waiting for me which would take two or three hours to reply before I could think of bed.

There were, however, occasional peaceful evenings when my wife and I could get up to the Sailing Club for a little relaxation. We all felt, I think, that it was merely the calm before the storm, and knew in our hearts that this was going to be one hell of a storm. The Japanese had invaded Burma at Mergui in the extreme south, but though there was still a long way for them to go, the sinking of the *Repulse* and *The Prince of Wales* on 10th December had been a very heavy blow to our self-confidence.

Then on the morning of 23rd December 1941, in broad daylight, the Japanese delivered their first air attack on Rangoon, most of the bombs falling on the densely populated eastern quarter near the assembly depots for the lorries for the Burma-China road. This quarter, populated mostly by labouring classes living in flimsy wooden buildings, was totally destroyed mainly by the subsequent fire, and casualties ran into four figures.

Indian refugees fleeing from Rangoon

Refugees on 180 mile walk from Rangoon to Prome

Almost before the planes were out of sight tens of thousands, loaded with all they could carry, or pushing their possessions on bicycles, rickshaws or every imaginable type of push cart, made for the open country north of the town. The Highway Code, traffic regulations and common sense all went by the board with this solid mass of humanity stretching from one side of the road to the other including the pavements, only intent on escaping from danger, danger which appeared very real with the roar of the planes and the dense smoke cloud so close behind them.

The commercial centre and poorer residential quarters in Rangoon covered a rectangular area about 1,000 yards in depth situated between the river and port in the south and the railway in the north. The nearest escape routes from this congested district were two bridges crossing the railway, one at the main station and the second about 600 yards to the east. These formed bottlenecks causing all approach roads to be packed with humanity till well on into the evening. To enter from the north by these bridges was practically impossible.

The crowd was composed mainly of Indians, the majority of whom intended to make for India as quickly as their feet would take them along the only route they knew. This route extended along the main Rangoon-Prome road for a hundred and eighty miles, then after crossing the Irrawaddy River bore westwards for about a hundred and ten miles across the Arakan Yomas via the Taungup Pass to Taungup, where river launches plied to Akyab, connecting with steamers for Chittagong and Calcutta. The minority made for the country outside the town, forming camps wherever shade and water were available. From these camps they intended to continue their normal duties until, at the first opportunity, they could board a ship for Madras or Calcutta. A few Chinese followed this minority. The Burmese who left sought sanctuary in the surrounding villages where they were sure of a welcome.

Before the Evacuation staff or the District authorities had time to assess the extent of the problem this exodus created, and almost before any remedial action could be taken, a second equally devastating raid on Christmas Day created additional panic and more than doubled the number of refugees. Accurate figures could not be obtained, but it is known that up to a hundred and fifty thousand arrived at Taungup whilst from 30,000 to 50,000 were dealt with in camps and settlements on the outskirts of Rangoon.

A very large proportion of these refugees were essential labour required in Rangoon, and it was therefore of vital importance to halt the stream of humanity along the Prome road and persuade them to return to the city. The Evacuation Department had hutted camps at the Race Course, at Chin Tsong's Palace and about ten miles out at Tanyingon, capable of accommodating about thirteen thousand. These camps were staffed and had adequate food supplies and cooking facilities. There were also a few rest camps along the Prome road at which refugees could spend the night, but would have to provide their own food.

As centres for the collection of refugees these camps proved of little use. Those who were prepared to reside near the city disliked any collection of huts which might be taken for military encampments and therefore bombed; they far preferred to stay under the trees. Several thousands camped round the Royal Lakes which, though in Rangoon, were north of the railway and were surrounded with densely wooded land providing the shade and cover they considered necessary. Then and in subsequent months it was noticed that the average refugee would consider himself far safer standing under trees and thus out of sight of the Japanese airmen than being in a trench exposed to the sky.

The most urgent work was to ensure adequate sanitation in these squatters' camps and along the

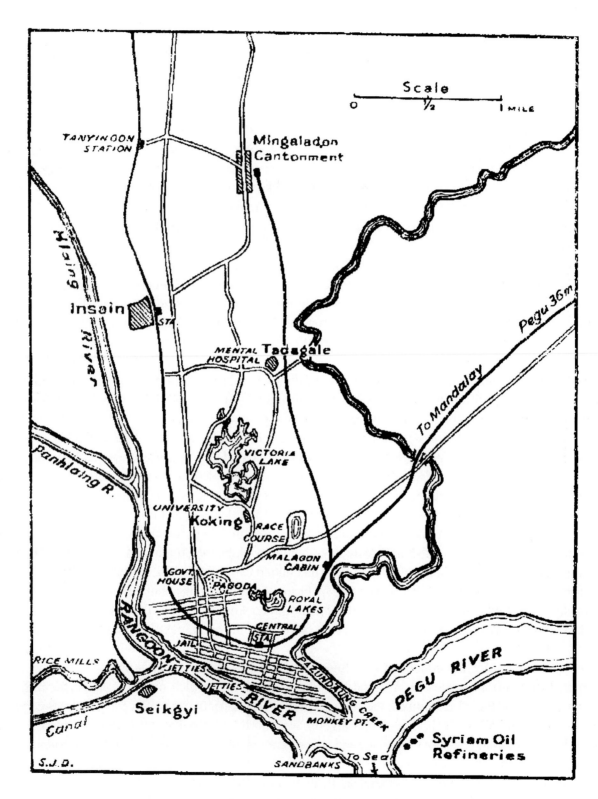

Map of Rangoon and its environs

Prome road, also to provide adequate food supplies. With the organisation ready at the three main camps it was not difficult to divert food supplies to food issue depots near groups of settlements, and to arrange for mobile food canteens to patrol routes out of the town. Over twelve thousand daily were fed by these canteens operating only within a few miles of the city.

The obstinacy of these people was at times infuriating. Having made their small camp, possibly only containing one family, there they insisted on staying, and no amount of persuasion would make them join up with other small groups in the vicinity. Sanitation and hygiene meant nothing to them. Their latrines would be the edges of the small ponds or lakes used as their water supply for both drinking and bathing. After a meal any food left over would be thrown on the ground, usually a few feet away from where they were sitting, creating conditions ideal for an epidemic of cholera. Fortunately the Public Health Department was a very efficient organisation and, with the help of evacuation staff posted to groups of camps, latrines were built and the refugees themselves encouraged to build their own huts with bamboo and thatch provided by my Department. Gradually we encouraged bazaar sellers to set up their stalls at these concentrations, many of which became thriving little settlements.

The refugees on the road came under the control of the District Authorities. At Prome these officials failed to prepare for such a complex emergency till it was too late. They were then faced with tens of thousands in the town and thousands more arriving daily, and had insufficient staff to cope with such numbers and no time to prepare an efficient evacuation plan for moving these crowds to Taungup. An attempt was made to limit the number crossing the river each day, but the very limited staff could not possibly apply such control, and before sufficient staff could be made available cholera broke out in the town and was carried by the refugees across the Pass to Taungup. Nothing could stop these Indians: they were attacked repeatedly along the Prome road by the Burmese and scores were murdered; they were short of food, they were told of the hardships of the Taungup Pass where(at 3,000 feet) water was very scarce, they were tired and weary before they left Prome, but they had made up their minds to get to India and no trials, tribulations or warnings could deter them. How many died or were killed along the Rangoon-Prome road is unknown, nor, I think, is there any record of the deaths in Prome, but it has been estimated that about three thousand died on the Taungup Pass.

No preparation had been made beforehand along this route, as it was known that at this time of year the available water supply over the Pass was quite inadequate for more than a few hardy travelers, whilst at Taungup the supply was limited to a few brackish wells. For miles the track wound its way through dense jungle up and down very steep slopes and with no habitation for days on end. It would have taken months of work to render this Pass fit for use as an evacuation route to India.

Evacuation Headquarters had a narrow escape on Christmas Day as a stick of bombs was dropped across the school site. All the staff were in the trenches, where I had intended going, but a zealous Anglo-Indian telephone operator on the direct line to the Civil Defence War room had refused to leave her post so I decided to keep her company. As the bombs were coming closer we moved into a central room – a sort of miniature school hall – and on hearing the whine of a probable direct hit I caught the girl by the scruff of the neck and hurled her to the floor; she was an attractive little thing and deserved far gentler treatment. A bomb seemed to explode in an adjacent room, immediately followed by a second just outside the wall. I had by then removed my nose from the hard ground and to this day swear I saw that wall bulge inwards and then to my relief straighten out again.

There were further crashes in the distance but more alarming was the crackle and roar of flames very close and we discovered that the cook house had got a direct hit and was blazing away, also the thatch roofed covered way from the main building to other buildings in the compound. That little telephone girl showed amazing pluck and in a few seconds found two four-gallon water tins and was trying to carry them to the fire. She was a thin slip of a thing, still trembling with fright and hardly had the strength to lift one tin, but refused to be beaten. Shortly after, the rest of the staff arrived to help.

I then discovered that two lorries loaded with full two-gallon petrol tins had driven into the gate as the raid started. The drivers, in no uncertain language, had been told to disappear. One lorry was last seen, so we heard later, about twenty miles away going as hard as it could up north; the other went a few yards up the road, received a direct hit, and lorry, petrol, driver and spare man vanished into thin air. Those were our only casualties, if one excludes a brand new pair of Simpson's (Piccadilly) daks which I was wearing for the first time in honour of Christmas and which were torn, burnt and completely ruined in the subsequent fire-fighting.

The objective of the raid had been the electric power station fairly close to the office, and as our house, also in the vicinity, had very narrowly missed a direct hit on the 23rd, I decided it was time for us all to move to a safer spot. We were fortunate in finding a palatial house almost in the shade of the Shwe Dagon Pagoda. The Japanese, being Buddhists like the Burmese, were certain to give this pagoda a wide berth in all their raids. The owner of the house, a very charming Chinese lady, left most of her furniture and we were able to house the entire office downstairs and use the upstairs as our own flat with spare rooms for several of my officers who now fed with us.

In 1945 when I returned to Rangoon I learned that the owner of that house had left hidden behind some loose bricks in a cupboard under the stairs jewellery to the value of over 50,000 rupees – about £3,500. During the Japanese occupation of Rangoon that house became the Headquarters of Aung San's rebel army, yet those jewels escaped discovery.

With all the refugee problem to tackle and the move of Headquarters, the staff problem also became very acute. As I had expected, resulting from the raids most of the schools closed down and the secretaries of many of the Government-aided and private schools responsible for paying the teachers disappeared, leaving my volunteers penniless. They had to be paid by someone or starve, and many of them had to be found accommodation as the second raid had destroyed a large Anglo-Indian quarter. I placed my proposals before Government, but the Defence expert was out of touch with the life of the Anglo-Indian and Anglo-Burman community and was against any suggestion of a paid staff. Some of these girls earned only about 70 to 100 rupees a month (about £5 - £7), and frequently one or two sisters were keeping a whole family. Government havered over my proposals; I went to several meetings with the authorities concerned, got tired of arguing so fixed scales of pay which I considered suitable and started a pay roll. In June of the following year, by which time we were in India, Government sanctioned those scales!

With many of the staff homeless and with the increasing difficulty in collecting them at all hours of the night and returning them to their homes, I requisitioned two more houses and started hostels for the staff close to the new Headquarters.

All this was only possible on the 24th. My small imprest account was absurdly inadequate to deal with the feeding and housing of the flood of refugees resulting from the raid on the 23rd, so I tackled the

Accountant General, a grand man and Commandant of my Race Course camp. He immediately took me along to the finance Minister, Sir Tun Aung Kyaw, and in less than an hour I came out of the Secretariat with a cheque book and authority to draw unlimited funds from the Reserve Bank. The next day, Christmas Day, the Bank Manager opened the bank specially on my behalf to cash my cheque for 20,000 rupees. If only all those in authority had had the contempt for red tape that these three gentlemen had, how much easier all our work would have been.

No reference to my staff would be complete without mention of the dispatch riders, about twenty schoolboys with bicycles on their Christmas holidays. To them it was a real lark and they enjoyed themselves, but we could not have done without them. They were of all ages, lived with their parents and used to report daily. They were full of mischief when not on a job and nearly frightened us out of our wits when we found them digging up what they thought was an unexploded bomb in the garden of our office. On another occasion, we found them busily digging out of a tree with penknives the phosphorous pellets from an anti-personnel bomb which had exploded nearby. One grand lad did brilliant work on the 25th helping to put out the fire at our office, and on the 23rd, immediately after the raid when our telephone lines were down, had taken a message to the War room in the centre of the town, managing to get through the hordes of refugees crossing the bridges. He was later awarded a Certificate of Honour from the Governor of Burma, and when I last saw him years later was a Captain in the Gurkha Rifles. I can well remember his disgust when his parents decided to take him to India on one of the last boats out of Rangoon. He so wanted to stay with us, and seriously discussed with me the chances of his disappearing temporarily on the day of embarkation. He, Kelly by name, and his extreme opposite, slow and stolid Bloxomb, were the mainstays of those lads.

Shortly after the raid of the 25th, the Governor of Burma formed what was generally known as the 'Soviet', a committee composed of heads of essential Government Departments and the large commercial concerns, who, under the Chairmanship of a senior Indian Civil Service official, met daily to deal with the ever-changing situation. Although it served its purpose, it was too unwieldy to authorize immediate action, snap decisions being completely foreign to many of the senior 'die-hard' officials. It was, however, often my only contact with other senior officers as there was no time for ordinary peace-time social visits.

After repeated requests to this Soviet, I obtained as my Deputy the services of T.C.D.Ricketts, a Forest Officer, and an ideal man for the job. Nothing tired him, he discussed matters with me each morning and I did not see him again till either late at night or early the next morning by which time everything needed would have been accomplished. When every twenty-four hours seemed twelve hours too short, it was a great relief to feel that I had at last one really competent man who could be trusted implicitly to cope efficiently with any emergency and accept responsibility.

I had been obliged to promote to officer rank some of the senior Anglo-Indians. They worked well but they, as schoolmasters, had never had to accept responsibility or make quick decisions and had not the self-confidence to make any definite decisions and act on them..

Another useful recruit was a Civil Servant from Borneo who was returning to that country on the expiry of his home leave. He was held up in Rangoon for some weeks and was posted to me, and proved most helpful. After the war I heard from him. He had been caught by the Japanese at Singapore and had spent the rest of the war in a prisoner of war camp.

Bomb damage near the Shwe Dagon Pagoda, Rangoon

CHAPTER II

For the next three weeks we were kept busy mainly with the Indian settlements. Though the Japanese in their two raids had only partially accomplished their object, mainly the disruption of the normal life of the city, so many of their planes had been shot down by the Royal Air Force and the American Volunteer Group that after the 25th December they confined their visits to the nighttime, and concentrated mainly on the airfields outside Rangoon, principally at Mingaladon.

We were unhindered, therefore, in our attempts to resettle this Indian labour. Efforts to persuade those on the road to return were not very successful, but the numerous settlements outside the town were gradually enlarged and formed into labour camps. Before Rangoon was evacuated in February, over twenty of such camps had been constructed, each to accommodate from five to eight hundred, and the occupants were transported daily to and from their centres of employment.

Demands for civil labour from the Army and Air Force were constantly increasing; and we were dispatching thousands to aerodromes and roads or up country for major military works. For this branch of our activities the schoolmaster staff were useless, having no experience of Indian labour, but I was fortunate in recruiting a number of European refugee rubber planters from Tenasserim and Mergui. About thirty of them arrived suddenly in Rangoon, most of them with only the clothes they stood up in, and some with wives and children. The unattached were only too pleased to join my staff, the others I housed at Government's expense at one of the main hotels until they could be sent off to India by boat. As always, one or two took advantage of the situation and threw the most terrific parties nightly to all their friends, the bills being presented to me at the end of the first week by the Hotel Manager. That had to be stopped, though months after when we got to India I repeatedly received demands from the hotel owners, who had also escaped, for expenditure incurred by these men.

Those that had joined my staff were splendid, one Green, an Australian not particularly amenable to discipline but who revelled in hard work, being given the task of starting the transport section. How successfully he accomplished that task will be told in a later chapter.

The Evacuation transport section was always a sore point with the authorities, who had formed a Civil Defence Transport pool from which we were expected to obtain our requirements. In theory this sounded satisfactory, in practice there was constant delay, as the pool never had sufficient vehicles to meet all demands. One or two of my staff had their own cars and we managed to scrounge an odd collection of vehicles, including old Burmese buses and broken down lorries, which Green with the help mainly of two Burmese mechanics got into running order. We hid this transport in a park in a side road under the shade of dense mango trees and gradually collected stocks of petrol, spare parts and vehicles, without which we should never have been able to feed the thousands in camps or provide the materials for the many camps under construction. We were, and probably still are being, accused of lack of co-operation, but without that transport we should never have been able to tackle the far bigger problem which confronted us in March and April.

The Officer in charge of the Civil Defence Transport pool was a most helpful Scot with a marvellous flow of language. On one occasion, in answer to my request over the phone for vehicles, he expressed his

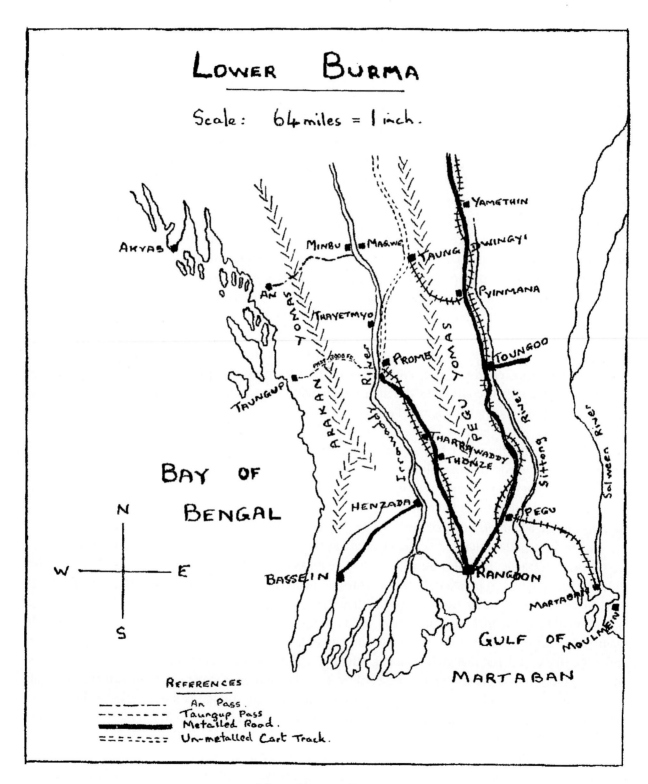

Map of Lower Burma

views on transport in general and authorities in particular in language which would have made the most hardened of bargees blush. He did not realise that there was an extension to my phone and that all conversations throughout each twenty-four hours were listened to and recorded by telephone operators. After this particular conversation I went out and apologized to the girl on duty, only to be told that she did not understand most of the words but some sounded lovely and she would try them out on the other girls in the hostel that night! This I gathered was their nightly equivalent to a bedtime story.

About this time a collection of Polish refugees turned up in Rangoon, having escaped from Poland via Russia, China, Hong Kong, Malay and now Burma. Government did not know what to do with them so passed them on to me. Some had their wives and children with them, some could hardly talk a word of English, and all were penniless. They were a grand crowd and would turn their hands to anything. One, an ex Le Mans racing driver, was given a lorry to drive and nearly terrified my wife out of her wits when taking her on a shopping expedition to the town. Shortly before Rangoon was evacuated I asked some of them to remain on my staff. Every one refused, as they had heard of a Polish Brigade being formed in Palestine and wanted to take an active part in the war. One or two specialists were sent to India for employment but the others all succeeded in joining their Army again.

During this period Japanese submarines appeared in the Gulf of Martaban and sank several of our merchant ships. The British officers and British, Chinese and Indian crews were brought into Rangoon and became my responsibility. For them we requisitioned a large house which had belonged to the Japanese Cotton Trading Company. It was beautifully furnished and was still in charge of the owners' Indian servants. These owners had all been interned, but before being taken away had given each servant 300 rupees and instructions to wait in the house for their return in three months' time. Within three months Rangoon had fallen and those Japanese cotton merchants were back in the house. It was significant that the finest dugouts in Rangoon, completely furnished and with electric light, were to be found in this house and at the house of the Japanese Consul nearby.

An extraordinary situation developed over these shipwrecked seamen. There was no charitable fund from which they could obtain money for the purchase of new clothes, nor had the Shipping Company's agents authority to disburse money for such purpose. Many of these men only possessed a torn vest and trousers, some of the Chinese and Indians had only a towel round their middle, yet nothing could cut through this red tape. There existed a war relief fund containing tens of thousands of pounds, but merchant seamen were not mentioned amongst the various classes for which it was raised. Eventually my Department had to produce the required funds, including the purchase of all bedding.

More Naval, Army and Royal Air Force personnel were arriving in Rangoon and at first there was some confusion over the requisitioning of buildings for their use. Each Arm had their own requisitioning authority, and buildings would be commandeered by both Navy and Air Force, the occupiers, in some cases Government Departments, not knowing where to go. When there was almost complete chaos, Government handed over all the requisitioning to the Evacuation Department; the Royal Air Force however refused to acknowledge our authority. I would be notified of the size of building required and my staff would then search the town. My wife and an American Baptist Mission Headmistress tackled this job.

One of the most persistent demands for safe accommodation came from a large Government Department housed near the docks. The Head of this Department was a very important gentleman, though not quite so important as he imagined, and he was exceedingly jittery. There was a lovely story going round of a visit he paid to Government House. Whilst interviewing His Excellency he suddenly blurted out: "Sirens", and dived under a table. After a few moments, the sound was traced to an adjacent room where the Governor's daughter was singing. Having at a distance heard that lady sing, I only hope she received the apology she more than deserved. On another occasion my wife and Miss Loughlin rang the bell of a large house which they considered might be suitable for the Army. Informing the owner of the reason for their visit, they discovered they were addressing the very infuriated Mayor of Rangoon, a Burman of considerable standing. At this time Burma had a Council of Ministers, mostly Burmans, and though war was at our gates it was essential that the co-operation and very friendly relations which existed between the European and Burmese officials should be maintained.

One incident connected with this requisitioning brought to light a most amazing racket being carried out by the Chinese responsible for getting lorries on to the Burma-China road. An important Chinese official in Rangoon called at my office to obtain a house for a member of the Chinese Government who had been sent to Rangoon to supervise the assembling of these vehicles. I enquired into the bona fides of this official and discovered that these lorries arrived from America in pieces and were taken over by a Chinese firm of motor engineers who then assembled the chassis and engine. They were then sold at a very handsome profit to another Chinese firm of body builders. On the completion of the body they were again sold, at a profit, to another firm owned by a Chinaman who was responsible for the wiring and fitting of all electrical appliances. This Chinaman was acting as secretary to the new official, who, as far as I can remember, called himself a commissioner. The secretary then sold the completed lorry, again at a very handsome profit, to the Chinese Government, who paid the commissioner a bonus for each lorry in running order placed on the road. From a reliable source I was told that the cost of these lorries to the Chinese Government worked out at approximately 40,000 rupees, equivalent to nearly £3,000. Again considerable tact was needed to convey to the Chinese officials that no accommodation was available.

News from the front was daily more depressing, and ever since the raid of the 25th December trains up country and boats to India had been packed. The two shipping companies mainly concerned were The British India and The Scindia Steam Navigation Company, and as the news got worse and the nightly raids more frequent the offices of these Companies were packed each day with hundreds of would-be passengers thronging the pavements and roadway outside, disorganizing all traffic. With such a demand and such a disorderly mob racketeering became a fine art. A purchaser had to pay the doorkeeper before entering the office, then the native shipping clerk demanded his share before issuing the ticket, pushing up the normal cost of 14 rupees to as much as 50 rupees or more. Frequently the purchaser would sell the ticket for twice what he paid as soon as he got out of the office. Later, as the Japanese got nearer Rangoon these tickets were sold in the bazaar for fantastic amounts.

This situation became so chaotic that Government placed the sale of deck passage tickets and embarkation in the hands of the Evacuation Department. It was, therefore, arranged that tickets would only be sold at the Race Course camp, where purchasers would reside until taken by lorries to the boats. On the first morning thousands mobbed the Course entrance. Expanded metal gates were knocked down and women and children were trampled on as the men, all Indians, clambered over the turnstiles. Inside the camp the staff were helpless, the crowds swarmed round, into and over the hut where tickets were to be sold. Everyone shouted, everyone fought to be first, and it became necessary to call on a Company of

Military Police, who with fixed bayonets herded the mob into the huts from where an orderly queue was organized; similar actions had to be taken on two later occasions.

To discourage able-bodied essential workers leaving, Government issued orders that only one male adult could accompany every five women and children. The Indian is no fool; he soon thought out a solution, and the number of women, regardless of age or looks, who earned an honest 20 rupees or more by becoming someone's wife, just long enough for the purchase of a ticket, must have run into well over a thousand. Children were hired out, and once having passed through the ticket office were whisked away – often with a new and strange 'Mother' – to the end of the line to make up another party of five for another male. Frequently extra tickets so obtained were thrown over the Race Course wall to a confederate outside who sold the ticket in the black market.

Under the orders in force luggage was limited to one suitcase or as much as each passenger could carry, yet the most amazing baggage was brought along. One woman, I remember, in addition to enormous bundles of clothing which she could only just lift, had tied to her body a large electric hair dryer, probably loot obtained after one of the air raids.

Racketeering was not confined to the purchase of tickets. Boats, which had been at anchor in midstream, would arrive alongside the docks with hundreds of refugees already on board. They had come down river on sampans and had climbed on to the boat via the anchor chains, paying a fee to the crew as they got on board.

All embarkation from the Race Course was carried out by night, the boats usually leaving in the following dawn. I would receive a message from the Naval Officer in charge in the afternoon, usually of this nature: "Tonight five boats available, embark three thousand between 10 p.m. and 4 a.m." Staff would then collect tickets from the Shipping Companies and proceed to the Race Course where they were sold. The Naval Officer had to be visited to find out the names of the boats, then the captains of those boats had to be interviewed, a time fixed for loading each, and a decision obtained on whether he required any additional supplies for feeding the refugees. Frequently we had to send bags of rice with the passengers. Transport had to be arranged and the Port Police contacted. Then from about 9.30 p.m. onwards a ghostly procession of Rangoon Electric Tramway Company's buses would be let out of the Race Course and, after a journey of about two miles, driven through one of only two gates at the docks in use at such times. Each bus would stop at the ship's gangway, would empty and be away, almost in seconds, through the other gate and back to the race Course for more passengers.

And so it went on hour after hour, night after night, frequently interrupted by air raid alarms and the sound of bombing and anti-aircraft guns in the direction of Mingaladon, sometimes closer. Then buses would have to be diverted away from the docks, or passengers on the docks rushed to basements in some of the large neighbouring houses. One never to be forgotten night there were seven air raid alerts and loading of one boat was within a few yards of a large dump of trench mortar shells and gelignite.

We on the staff welcomed these alerts. It was very hot and thirsty work, as we had to live like dogs with a herd of sheep. The docks were dark as pitch, frequently owing to cargo the buses could not get to the gangways and passengers had to be unloaded yards away and led through a maze of crates, wires ropes and machinery to their boat. If it was possible to lose their way, they did, and invariably some were attempting to take with them more than they could carry and would suddenly disappear to collect a box they had left at the bus. During those breathing spaces caused by an alert we would dash back to the house, or across to the Silver Grill for a whiskey and soda. At times we had been on this embarkation for two or three nights running and had been at work most of the day. But for the whiskey we should have fallen asleep. One sweated like a pig and every drink one had came out immediately in the form of perspiration.

The Silver Grill was the only decent night club going full blast till the early hours, and was always packed to capacity; Pete Arratoon, the ex-boxer owner, had the most amazing knack of keeping order even when drink had been flowing very freely amongst a very mixed racial clientele. I often wonder whether Pete ever got out of Burma the small fortune he must have made at this time; I hope so, as his unfailing courtesy, good humour and excellent service during a period when servants were disappearing without warning, and when tempers were decidedly frayed, well deserved all that Dame Fortune could shower on him.

All records of this sea evacuation were subsequently lost, but figures taken at Indian ports show nearly seventy thousand arrivals from Burma at that time, mostly Indians. It was at times heartbreaking to see boats leaving empty, but these were mostly cargo boats with steel decks on which it would have been cruelty to have embarked deck passengers, particularly as such ships had inadequate water storage space for passenger traffic. Some passenger boats did escape us and I have never been able to find out if that was the fault of the Naval Authorities for failing to give us the name of the ships, or their Captains who disliked having their command messed up by hundreds of refugees. One of the largest boats ever to come alongside in Rangoon – a French 'President' liner – got away empty. I was at the docks that night, having been given the names of five boats to load, and heard that this ship was at the end of the line. By the time I got to her the mooring ropes had just been cast off and an ever-widening gap was appearing at the dockside. She was completely empty and could have carried several thousands.

At the Race Course the camp had to be cleared periodically and cleaned out as the refugees were the worst type of litterbugs and they would insist on using the slit trenches as latrines. Several casualties were caused during these 'spring cleanings' when the staff swept up two cigarette tins which had been made into bombs. This was undoubtedly fifth column activity to create panic, and thus disorganise the life of the town and the port on which the army completely depended for its supplies and reinforcements.

The finding, and on the 22nd February the loading, of the last boat is a fantastic story which readers may find hard to believe. Some weeks earlier there was the danger of the departure of all the staff of the Soortie Burra Bazaar, the main food supply centre in Rangoon. The Food Controller, to quell the alarm, obtained from me boat tickets which he issued to the leaders as a guarantee that all would be evacuated to India, but on the understanding that they would only go when he gave permission. It was an agreement made in all good faith, but a dangerous one, and one which unfortunately could not eventually be honoured in full. I had made a similar agreement with all the sweepers and water carriers at the General Hospital and Dufferin Hospital.

On the 21st a convoy arrived with, amongst other troops, the Armoured Brigade, the first armour our Army had received. Hearing that this would be the last convoy I went to the docks to see how many boats would be available. The sight of those troops, the 4th Hussars, manhandling their tanks off those boats, put new heart into one. All dock labourers, including the crane drivers, had disappeared, and those bronzed men, straight from North Africa, and bare to the waist, were pushing those tanks about as if they

Sir Reginald Dorman-Smith, Governor of Burma, with General Alexander,
Commander of the Army Group in Burma, 1942

FOOTNOTE:
    There is a popular misunderstanding - also implied in this book - that the British and
Commonwealth troops defending Burma at the time of the Japanese invasion were the XIV Army.

    In March, 1942 General Slim only had under his command one Burma Corps consisting of
two Divisions (17th Indian and 1st Burma) as part of the Burma Army commanded by General
Alexander which included the Chinese V and VI Armies, each corresponding roughly to a British
Army Corps.

    The XIV Army - a much larger force altogether - was not created until October, 1943 under
the command, from its inception, of General Slim. The fact that it was he, at different times, who
was in command of these very different sized forces probably accounts for this misunderstanding.

were toys. As soon as one landed on the docks, the engine would start and it would roar away through the dock gates. It was a magnificent sight.

Most of the ships were cargo boats with steel decks, undoubtedly few water storage tanks and unlikely to be suitable for passengers. I continued searching and saw the Scindia boat, the S.S. *Jalligopal* coming alongside at the Company's jetty. Arriving at the office of the Naval Officer in charge to find out what ships would be allocated for evacuees, I was kept waiting in an anteroom for over half an hour, though there was no one with the officer I normally interviewed on such matters. This was not unusual as this particular gentleman was noted for his discourtesy and I had several times at previous interviews had to keep a strict hold of my temper. I had even more difficulty this time on being told that there were no boats available and the *Jalligopal*, which we could see from his office window, was not arriving, having been diverted to India.

There was no arguing with the man, so I rushed off to the *Jalligopal*, saw the Captain and got his agreement to wait until 9 p.m. He would not give me a moment after that hour as it was the last chance of catching the tide. I had the dock gates locked and obtained his promise to load no one till I brought my own bus loads of bazaar merchants and hospital servants. There followed a frantic three hours, getting transport collected, warning the bazaar and the hospitals and arranging for all to be picked up at the General Hospital. Ricketts I sent to the *Jalligopal* to supervise embarkation. At 8 p.m. the first lorries were just moving off when he returned with the news that the ship had left. The Indian Agent of the Company had decided to leave, had had the dock gates opened, loaded the boat with about two thousand Indians who had been clamouring round the gates and had ordered the Captain to up anchor.

I could have murdered anybody I was so furious, so, getting the buses empty and all the disappointed occupants back to their homes, I made for Government House where I demanded an interview with His Excellency Sir Reginald Dorman-Smith. Almost immediately I was called upstairs to find the Governor talking with a very tall, typically Naval, Commodore. I blurted out my complaint, 'blurted' is I fear the only appropriate word, only to be informed that this Commodore was the newly-appointed Naval Officer in charge. After further discussion when I became more coherent His Excellency finally requested the Commodore to go with me to the docks then and there and find a ship for me. His Excellency the Governor planned to visit the Police Headquarters that night and ordered us to report to him there at 11 p.m.

En route to the docks we collected Tony Hobson of Mackinnon Mackenzies, the Agents of the British India Steamship Company. Tony had been the Company's representative at all the embarkation I had carried out and had been of invaluable assistance. The Commodore took us direct to the Naval Mess where we had a few 'words' with the officer I had met that afternoon, and who now denied all knowledge of our earlier conversation. The Commodore tactfully poured oil on very troubled waters by supplying Tony and me each with a carton of much needed cigarettes, and we then set off for the docks. This visit to one section of the docks was fruitless, and after reporting our failure to His Excellency at the Mogul Guard, at 11 p.m. we returned to continue the search.

It was by then very dark but as we entered the dock gates, which were open and unguarded, we passed two Burmese buses driven by Burmese drivers coming out packed with service rifles. At the docks pandemonium reigned; unloading had been completed, the crew had come ashore and, finding enormous stocks in the warehouses of Australian wine and beer, were indulging in a Bacchanalian orgy almost beyond description. There was not a single man sober, they were rolling, staggering, some crawling, some flat out dead drunk. Shots were being fired through the roof, anywhere, by drunkards who had found rifles and ammunition, the noise of smashing bottles was continuous.

We went to the first gangway at which stood a bearded and very unsteady Merchant Service Quartermaster. As the Commodore started to mount the gangway, the Quartermaster caught him a crack across the chest, remarking: "You can't bloody well come up 'ere." Hearing some remarks from one of us that with a drunken article like this on the gangway no wonder everyone was in the same state, this bearded old salt turned very unpleasant and, using the most appalling language, shouted out: "Me, a drunken article; I've served thirty —, —, — years before the —, —, — mast which is more than any of you b——s have ever done", at the same time landing another crack across the Commodore's chest. Discretion was obviously indicated, so we moved on to the next boat. There was no guard on the gangway but there was a most unpleasant smell of pears. The Naval Lieutenant with us attempted to go on board but he soon discovered the smell was caused by tear gas, forcing him to return. In a shouted conversation with the officers who were marooned in their cabins at the bridge level, we understood some of the crew had come on board fighting drunk and, hitting each other about with bottles, had smashed some containing tear gas and not drink as they imagined, rendering the main decks uninhabitable.

We moved on and, after finding a suitable ship, returned to Government House with the news, where I arranged with the Commodore to have all my passengers at the docks at 8 a.m. the next morning, when he very kindly promised to be present.

That meant another two hours or so making arrangements, and before 8 a.m. the first bus loads drew up alongside this boat. Before the Commodore arrived a senior officer from Army Headquarters appeared and requisitioned the ship, refusing to accept His Excellency's authority in allocating it to me. Shortly after he disappeared the Commodore turned up; he had already heard of the Army's action but was good enough to allow me to load three hundred of my refugees. The remainder unfortunately had to be sent away. Whilst we were embarking the three hundred more trouble appeared, as the crowds of a thousand or more broke through the dock gates and rushed the gangway. There followed an amazing scene. I had about six or eight of my staff with me, all fortunately with sticks, whilst most of the newcomers were carrying large boxes on their heads. A slight poke in their tummies with the sticks and they doubled up, their boxes fell to the ground, and that halted them as no Indian will, if he can possibly help it, leave his possessions. However, for about half an hour it was an unpleasant business, particularly as many of the hospital servants and bazaar merchants had brought their wives and children, who were in grave danger of being pushed into the river between the dockside and the ship. Eventually the crew had to cut the ropes and let the gangway crash on to the dockside.

We returned to the buses and took those passengers left to the railway station and got them on a train to Prome.

The night before this crisis the officer dealing with the sailing of first and second-class passengers had paid us a visit, as he often did. He frequently obtained advance information of the arrival of boats and on this particular occasion told me of the expected arrival of the *Jalligopal* on the following morning. Frequently I was given information by my staff, who had heard the news in the local bazaars, of the names of boats with the actual dates of sailing from Calcutta long before the Naval authorities in Rangoon had, so they said, heard anything. How the bazaars received this news was a mystery as there was a strict censorship on telegrams.

The morning the *Jalligopal* was expected my office was besieged by scores of first and second-class passengers, complaining that the office at which they had been told to report to receive their tickets was shut and that the officer had left Rangoon. After a visit to the office concerned I found this was correct, the particular gentleman having presumably lost his nerve. I later paid my usual visit to Government House, when His Excellency, after telling me the news that Rangoon was to be evacuated, asked me if I knew where this officer had gone. On replying in the negative, I received orders to arrest him wherever I might find him. At least three weeks later I met him in Maymyo safely ensconced in another nice job.

On an earlier occasion, after spending the whole night loading ships, I returned to my Headquarters only to find another crisis. The Commandant at the Palace Camp had for hours been on the telephone demanding my presence. My wife who had answered the phone was convinced he was drunk. Driving to the camp, I found the Commandant, an Anglo-Indian, very drunk and surrounded by an impressive pile of empty bottles. He demanded the dismissal of all his staff who had been trying to suppress him. After settling the affair and appointing temporarily a new Commandant, I was hailed as I was leaving by a party of Anglo-Indian refugees housed in the main hall of this enormous Palace. I found I was required to hold the hand of a lady who was in the throes of childbirth – an entirely new experience for me. When that was over and as I was driving away from the building, the deposed Commandant, still very drunk, jumped on my car and started to protest. I have never in my life enjoyed so much pushing out a straight right and seeing a man fly backwards and go out for the count.

The day before loading up that last boat I had my first contact with a war correspondent. He had arrived on one of the boats in the convoy and represented, so far as I remember, a well-known English daily paper, also an American one. He appeared at my office very early in the morning and asked for a story. Not having time to relate all that had happened, I suggested he should spend the day with me, see what we were doing, and I could answer all his questions as we went about. During the morning we visited Government House and arrived at the A.D.C.'s office to find the Military Secretary at his desk with a glass of beer, one A.D.C., who had been on duty the previous night, fast asleep on the sofa, and a second A.D.C. enjoying a pink gin. Shortly after, His Excellency appeared, and after discussing with him the situation, we left. Finding he could not send a cable from the Telegraph Office the correspondent decided to return to India, and I dropped him at the docks to re-embark on the boat on which he arrived. Nearly three years after, I was shown a cutting from a 1942 newspaper reporting a tour of Rangoon carried out by this war correspondent with a 'Dr. Vorley', relating how on arriving at Government House we had found the staff cleaning and oiling their revolvers and tommy guns. Shortly after, a Sikh Havildar of the Governor's Bodyguard marched in, so the story went, and reporting that hundreds of armed rioters were attacking Government House, asked for the tommy guns. These were handed to him and there followed several bursts of firing. After a while, the Havildar returned and reported the dispersal of the rebels, on which the A.D.C. promised he would receive a reward for his gallant action.

I have yet to meet again that war correspondent, but would like to, if only to tell him that my faith in newsprint has never been the same since.

We were fortunate in that not a single boat containing refugees was attacked or sunk and, as far as I know, not a single casualty resulted from embarkation. Some of the voyages must have been sheer hell,

Rangoon street with Sule Pagoda

Rangoon deserted after evacuation order of February 20th, 1942

particularly one of a boat set aside especially for Anglo-Indians and Anglo-Burmans and the better-class Indians, more than two thousand eight hundred of whom were embarked. As I watched the boat leaving the jetty there was hardly room on the decks for passengers to sit down. I heard later that many during the four-day voyage were unable to find space to lie down.

An incident occurred connected with the departure of this boat which will illustrate the courage and loyalty of the female members of my staff. It was then towards the end of January 1942, there had been no halt in the Japanese advance, and it was almost certain that we should be unable to hold Rangoon. Once that town fell our only escape route to India was overland, and there was no known direct route. I called up all these women, and, explaining the situation to them, gave them a chance of leaving by this boat. I had to tell them I could not guarantee once Rangoon fell that anyone would get to India, but could only promise them that if I could get there they would be with me. The night before my wife and I had discussed this and she had refused to leave me, which information I passed on to these girls. One, and one only, decided to leave, but later she was joined by her great friend. All the rest insisted on remaining; I little realised then how much that decision was going to mean. We could never have accomplished what we did in the subsequent months without the help of the female staff; they were truly wonderful.

An additional headache with this embarkation was the Government of Burma's insistence that everyone must pay for his ticket. Many could not pay, particularly a large crowd of Indians who arrived from Moulmein. They had started over a thousand strong but en route, walking the whole way – nearly two hundred miles – they had been constantly attacked by the Burmese, and only about three hundred survived to turn up one day at the Palace camp. They were utterly destitute, many were wounded and all had the most ghastly tales of atrocity and murder, which quickly demoralised the other occupants of the camp. It was vital that they should be shipped to India as quickly as possible, but Government refused to permit the issue of free tickets. The Government of India eventually solved the impasse by guaranteeing payment, and from that day we used our own discretion in issuing free tickets to destitutes.

This attitude of the Government may be hard to understand, but it must be remembered that the Burmese Ministers were very averse to spending money on behalf of these non-indigenous people. Shortly after taking over the embarkation of deck passengers I had suggested to Government that it should be compulsory for all elderly women and women with children, of any race, to leave by boat for India. I was told that such an order would create despondency and alarm and would therefore be most inadvisable. That was typical of the general attitude as no one, except possibly the very 'high ups' in the Government, knew how serious was the military position. I remember early in February asking the Governor if he had any idea how long we had left to evacuate people by boat. He told me that he had been unable to obtain from the Army any detailed appreciation of the military situation.

In addition to evacuation by boat and train, many of the Europeans were leaving by air. This was not under my control, but the Royal Air Force Squadron Leader in charge was a great friend of ours and frequently came to visit us in the evenings. Government had ruled that first priority by plane would be given to expectant mothers, and this Royal Air Force officer gave us many a laugh in repeating the names of the 'Sarahs' who had flown out that day. Some elderly husbands must have had very unpleasant surprises in Rangoon, only to have cause to believe almost in miracles when they met their wives, slim waisted again, when they themselves arrived in India. I fear there must have been a boom in the sale of small air pillows during that air evacuation.

By the middle of February there was little cause for optimism and I was beginning to worry about keeping my female staff in Rangoon. The Japanese had crossed, or were crossing the Sittang river, and that meant the main Rangoon-Mandalay road and railway line being cut off before very long. On the 17th I heard that the Japanese were nearing Pegu, only fifty-four miles from Rangoon. The truth was not quite as bad as that, though we did not know it at the time. It was obviously advisable for these women to leave, so they, with a school from Thaton, were sent off by train on the following morning. An amusing little incident occurred at the station just before they entrained. As we entered the station, the sirens sounded. There were no trenches very near so my wife and I sat in the station hall on her bedroll, both feeling far from cheerful. We could hear bombs dropping away in the distance when a jeep suddenly tore up to the station and out stepped Booth Russell, one of my staff and ex rubber planter. Nothing ever worried him, and joining us on the bedroll he proceeded to take out of his pockets packet after packet of sweets and chocolates. It was the sort of absurd situation we needed to lift us out of our depression.

After picking up an orphanage at Kyauktaga the train stopped for breakfast the next morning at Pyinmana where the Japanese, mistaking it for a Chinese troop train, bombed it three times. Miraculously all the children escaped, but there were several casualties amongst my staff, which my wife will relate in a subsequent chapter. Some time on the 20th the Traffic Manager of the Railway told me he had heard that the train had been bombed but had no details, and it was not till the morning of the 23rd that a man walked in to my office and remarked, "Are you Mr. Vorley? I was given this note by Mrs. Vorley at Pyinmana but had not time to come along and give it to you." This was a note to tell me she was safe.

As evidence of the efficiency of the Japanese intelligence system, the day after this train was bombed Tokyo radio apologized for bombing a refugee train which they thought was a Chinese troop train.

Up till about the 20th trains were still leaving Rangoon for both Mandalay and Prome. They were always packed and we had Evacuation staff at the stations helping to control the crowds. Government Departments were moving up country and if any of our transport was spare we helped to move all their staff and records from offices and houses to the trains. Every day the uncertainty, the hustle and the worry became more acute, and there seemed to be no time for rest or sleep. One morning started off with a visit from the Roman Catholic priest in charge of the leper Asylum, a grand Frenchman, who was most indignant when I refused his request to evacuate his patients. Any car, boat or train used for such purpose would require thorough disinfection afterwards, and this was not possible. Shortly after he left the telephone rang and I was asked to evacuate the Zoo. That I also refused.

Then on the 20th February, 1942, orders were received to evacuate Rangoon, only the last ditchers remaining behind to blow up and destroy installations such as the refinery, mills etc. It was only by chance that I heard of these orders. Some time before, the military and civil authorities had prepared an evacuation scheme for those who were obliged to remain in Rangoon to the last moment, but this scheme in its entirety had not been made known to me. I was aware that there should be a special train for women employed at Military Headquarters and for nurses and other civil female employees. I had also been issued with large labels on which was printed the letter 'E'. These labels were to be pasted on the windscreen of our cars when evacuation orders were received, and would entitle one to draw petrol from the Government pumps, the only pumps which would then be operating. Early on the morning of the 20th I paid my usual visit to Government House and noticed these labels on all the Government House cars. Talking to His Excellency, I rather gathered he was preparing to leave, and on enquiring was only then informed that the orders for evacuation had been issued very early that morning. After giving me various instructions, the Governor told me to stay on in Rangoon until I could be of no further use, i.e. until there was no further hope of getting anybody away by boat or train.

We were kept busy up till the afternoon of the 23rd loading trains and the only boat we could get, and were then informed by the Naval and Railway authorities that no more boats or trains would be available for civilians. Trains for some days had been running a shuttle service from Rangoon-Tharrawaddy and from Tharrawaddy-Prome, and wherever possible we had issued food to occupants of camps and had advised them to start off on the walk up the road to Prome.

For over a week the banks had been closed and I had been obliged to keep in the office all the takings from the sale of passage tickets. These had gradually mounted up to the large sum of 87,000 rupees, equivalent to over £6,000. This money was in coin and notes of small denomination, the largest being 10 rupees. Being far too bulky to keep in the office safe, it had been put into a large rice sack and before my wife left had been kept in her wardrobe behind her frocks. Now with this sudden order to evacuate the town this money was a blessing as no one knew when we should get in touch with a bank again.

During the last three days Green had been busy scrounging every vehicle he could lay his hands on, one being the Turf Club ambulance which we heard had been taken by an important Burmese gentleman who had loaded it with all his personal belongings and was about to disappear. We just caught him in time. We also collected three Rangoon Electric Tramway Company's Diesel-engined passenger buses, a Polson's coffee van and several lorries. One of these lorries, which had been ours originally, we discovered outside a certain gentleman's house, loaded up with his Frigidaire, the contents of his extensive wine cellar, and a good deal of his furniture, and he and his friend were on the point of departure for the Shan States.

Conditions in Rangoon during those last three days were very far from pleasant. Due to an unfortunate misinterpretation of orders, the gates of the asylum and the Rangoon jail had been opened and lunatics and jailbirds were roaming the town. The latter had for a while the time of their lives looting and setting fire to the shops until the Police had orders to open fire on anyone caught in the act. It was at times quite hair-raising driving through the town, as one never knew when a shot would whiz past one, often I think fired by the looters themselves who had managed to collect arms and ammunition. The lunatics were comparatively harmless; I remember seeing one, stark naked as the day he was born, perched up a tree in Windermere Crescent, the normal home of all the most senior Government officials. He told me he was on his way to Moulmein, only about two hundred miles away and well behind the Japanese lines.

All during the morning of the 23rd my staff had been busy sorting out the records and files and collecting essential clothes and kit which they would take away with them. Old and useless vehicles we had sabotaged and by about three o'clock in the afternoon we were ready to leave. It was a severe wrench to walk out of the house and leave most of our possessions, in my case the collection of nearly twenty years . My wife had been able to send on one of the last boats two steel and two wooden uniform cases with, very fortunately, our English winter clothes, my collection of ivory carvings and a few pieces of family silver, but rugs, carpet, furniture, linen and all our other possessions had to be left behind. One of our party, a newly-married young officer, remembered after we had gone about four miles that he had left a photo of his wife on his dressing table; he rushed back only to find the looters already in the house, removing everything they could carry.

I returned to that house in 1945 hoping to retrieve some of my possessions, but could only find a much scratched padauk dressing table minus the mirror and drawers. Apart from a token payment of 1,000 rupees (£70) or one month's pay, whichever was less, on arrival in India some months later, a 'generous' Government is now (1950) going to make an ex gratia payment of £450 as compensation; this is about one tenth, at present day prices, of what we lost. This has since been revoked (1951) because I have accepted a job overseas in the Commonwealth.

As we drove out of Rangoon, many parts of it burning, it was pitiful to see race horses worth thousands of rupees wandering about the roads, grazing on the grass edges, whilst at the Race Course where we stopped to load up supplies from the main Civil Supply dump, several of these animals, roaming loose, came whinnying up to us for food.

Passing the Race Course, we came to a refugee camp the occupants of which the day before had been given five days' supplies and told to take the road to Prome. We found them still in the camp clamouring for more food; they had sold all that had been issued to them to the surrounding Burmese villagers. Back we went to the Race Course, filled several lorry loads – there were over eight hundred of these refugees – and issued out another five days' supply.

We were all very worn out, all of us had been working night and day without regular sleep for weeks; if one had managed to get to bed at a fairly reasonable hour, which was very rare, the sirens or the anti-aircraft guns in the vicinity would drive sleep away. The reaction of feeling that it was all over and that it was now possible to relax physically and, even more welcome, mentally, made it difficult to concentrate on driving along a road swarming with refugees. After about ninety miles we gave up the unequal contest and, driving into the compound of a rice mill near Thonze, threw ourselves on to the hard concrete drying floor, and there slept the clock round.

To those reading about these incidents so many years after it may at first appear as if the administration and organisation in Rangoon at that time was far from efficient and decidedly lacking in foresight. It must be remembered that no one anticipated the Japanese advance would be so rapid and, as can be seen from the map on page 10, that within one month they would occupy the whole of Tenasserim Division and move westwards to occupy Rangoon. A Chinese Army some time earlier had come to our aid, and with the Salween and the Sittang rivers between us and the enemy after Moulmein had fallen, all of us expected the pace of the Japanese advance to slow down considerably, if not to be actually halted. Few of us knew that there was little, if any, truth in the repeated assurances in the Press of the adequacy of our Air Force strength. I have been told that the Chinese offer of assistance was at first rejected by the Burmese Government as the Burmese Ministers were nervous that once the Chinese got into Burma we should never get them out. That is more than possible, as the Chinese have always wanted an outlet in the Gulf of Martaban. There was also a story going round that the Army would not tell the Civil Government the whole truth of the situation as they did not trust the loyalty of the Burmese Ministers. That again is more than possible as the late U Saw was not the only Minister who was suspected of being in communication with the enemy. On the other hand, some of the Ministers were absolutely loyal. Two, I think possibly three, were undoubtedly responsible for stopping another rebellion early in 1942 in the Tharawaddy District. If that had occurred none of us, including the Army, would probably have ever reached India.

Once the Japanese started raiding Rangoon conditions changed almost daily, and the slightest rumour spread like wildfire through the bazaars and caused another problem. The organisation could undoubtedly have been better, given more time and more information, but it could have been infinitely worse, and unlike so many tragedies which had occurred in Malaya, practically everyone who wanted to leave Rangoon and could leave the town, got out. There was little panic; even the hordes who left the town after the raids of the 23rd and 25th December were, once across the two main bridges, a determined orderly crowd, and all praise is due to the last ditchers, who so thoroughly carried out a scorched earth policy before they left.

CHAPTER III

BY

HELEN VORLEY

My husband and I were so often separated during the hectic and chaotic six months of 1941-1942 covered by this book, and had such exciting, and often nerve-racking, experiences of which he knows very little, that we decided the history of the evacuation would be incomplete without my narrative. Further, having read through my husband's draft, I think there may be numerous incidents in the daily life of the staff of the Department which might be of particular interest as seen through a woman's eyes.

Prior to arriving in Rangoon in March 1941 I had spent the preceding five months on tour with him examining all the foothills south of Yamethin, covering on foot about three hundred miles.

After getting settled in a small furnished bungalow I was anxious to find some sort of war work, but as the war fever had by then hardly reached the East, it was some time before I found I could be usefully employed in the cutting out department of the Burma War Comforts Association controlled by a friend of mine. This organisation was extremely well run, garments being cut out and sent complete with buttons to up country stations, where they were finished and returned to the central Depot. At this Depot a senior lady controlled each of the many departments, which included knitting, cutting out, children's clothes for bombed-out victims, packing and, most important of all, buying the material. The buyers were mainly Indian ladies who managed to obtain incredible amounts of cloth. My weekly outturn of about 100 yards included surgeons' coats, pyjamas, bed jackets, shirts, vests and pants. Most of the made-up garments were sent to England, but stocks kept in Rangoon later proved most necessary for the air raid casualties and for merchant seamen who had been torpedoed.

At the end of July we moved to a larger house and had living with us a young Indian Civil Service officer who had recently taken in the United Kingdom a course in Air Raid Precautions. He was posted to the Civil Defence Department in Rangoon and asked me to become one of his 'girls' to train as a telephone operator, instruction being given three evenings each week. Most of the others were Anglo-Indian or Anglo Burman school teachers, stenographers and shop assistants, but they were all grand girls and we had some very amusing times together. The instruction was held at the Mogul Street Police Headquarters in a very small room containing about twenty telephones. The noise and heat were appalling. We had to write each message down as it was delivered and, as most of the Wardens were non-European, their pronunciation of the English language was at first extremely difficult to follow.

In October a 'Forces Club' was opened, a much needed institution. A large disused nursing home was acquired and was furnished mainly through the generosity of the large commercial houses in Rangoon. These firms were most lavish in their gifts, supplying a refrigerator, wireless sets, tables, chairs, a billiard table, dart boards, china, glass, in fact everything that was needed.

The Club was open from 5 p.m. to 11 p.m. every day and, except for three Indian cooks, was staffed by volunteers from the European community. After the two daylight raids on Rangoon in December all the Indian staff decamped and I arrived one evening to find only about three other women there. Two of us spent the evening frying enormous amounts of sausages, potatoes, eggs and bacon, and I think managed to maintain the excellent standard of cooking the canteen had prided itself on up till then. To those unaccustomed to a charcoal range in a kitchen without a fan and in a tropical climate, the heat we had to contend with that night is difficult to imagine.

There were no trenches near the club and the air raid shelters were across the road. The volunteer helpers during a raid sought refuge in the store cupboard under the stairs which was ten times worse than in the kitchen.

Until the Japanese declared war life was rather monotonous and humdrum. There would be cutting out at the Central Depot three mornings a week, two mornings of female bridge, three evenings a week training to be a telephone girl and the rest of the time taken up in the normal duties of running a house, exercising the dogs and looking after a husband.

Then on 8th December we were disturbed at an early hour by the telephone, and my husband rushed off to his office where he was now Director of Civil Evacuation, Rangoon. I took his breakfast down to him and, offering to do any job that was needed, spent the next two or three days sitting at a desk whilst the girls on the staff were busy helping to evacuate the Blind School and the Deaf and Dumb and other schools. I found these days very trying, as a constant stream of people kept rushing in and out asking all sorts of impossible questions, most of which I could not answer. By the end of the week the office was properly organised and we worked in three eight-hour shifts.

I became one of the telephone girls. There was an extension from the Director's telephone on which two girls were always on duty. Every message was written down on forms like telegraph forms, pink for incoming, white for outgoing, the time of the conversation being recorded. One girl used to be at the end of the phone, often for half an hour at a time making rough notes of every message sent or received. Whilst she deciphered theses notes and wrote out the messages on the appropriate forms the second girl would take over the phone. If the Director was out, as frequently occurred for hours on end, these forms were attached to separate boards for 'In' and 'Out' and handed to him when he returned. Later they were all filed and became most useful references, as life was so hectic it was impossible to remember all the communications and matters of importance these messages dealt with.

On the morning of the 23rd December we had just finished a late breakfast and I was going off to my last morning's bridge when the Air Raid sirens sounded. Our Indian Civil Service guest rushed off to his office and later had a 'grandstand' view of the raid, hiding behind a chimney pot on the roof of the Law Courts. I was hesitating what to do when the sirens sounded the 'all clear'. I got into the car and later was very surprised to see some Chinese crouching under a tree beside the road, all looking very terrified. Very shortly after my Burmese driver started talking very excitedly and, looking in the direction where he was somewhat wildly pointing, I saw a Japanese plane coming down in flames with the pilot bailing out. On arriving at my destination, we delayed our bridge to watch events from a small hill in the garden. The raid continued until 2 p.m., and in between the arrival of each separate wave of Japanese planes we attempted bridge, but the play was very wild, most of us revoked and all of us scattered to the trenches whenever the bombs started to fall; all of us except one who, crippled with rheumatism, could only get as far as the downstairs lavatory under the stairs.

On arriving home I found that an anti-personnel bomb had burst in the road by our front gate killing a number of Indian coolies. The electric current was off and on going upstairs I found the bedroom and bathroom as if a cyclone had hit them. All the bottles and other moveable objects were on the floor, most of them broken, and the mess was incredible. My little wire-haired terrier, always rather nervous and disliking noises, had disappeared, but to my relief was returned next day by a doctor living a few doors down the road. From then on the servants had orders to put the dogs on leads as soon as the sirens sounded; this was soon unnecessary as the dogs became so cute they made for the trenches on their own directly they heard the sirens and jumped out when they heard the 'all clear'.

The 24th was peaceful but the town was so disorganised that most of the large shops were closed. They opened on the 25th and that morning I went into the town to do my Christmas shopping for a dinner party we were giving all the girls on the staff that night. Only one of the owners was in attendance at the main store and shoppers helped themselves to what they needed, piled everything on the counter and then waited for him to come along and work out the bill.

Just as I got back to the office at about noon the sirens went and my husband advised me to wait awhile before returning to the house. The War Room at Civil Defence Headquarters kept us informed by phone of the whereabouts of the planes, and after about a quarter of an hour I was ordered to take all the staff to the trenches which were very shallow and completely uncovered. No sooner were we in the trenches than two lorries laden with two-gallon tins of petrol drew up on the other side of the hedge. We all yelled to the drivers to move on and one drove his vehicle just down the road where it received a direct hit and went up in a terrific blaze.

Nothing happened for some time after we were in the trenches, and getting bored, I was just about to go across to the office and find out if there was any news when we heard the planes. Our own had been about all the morning and one of the girls was standing up counting them; she had got up to thirty when we realised they were Japanese, as they were flying in a perfect 'V' formation, a habit of theirs. We all flattened ourselves in the trenches and hoped for the best. It was all hell let loose for about five minutes. I got a piece of incendiary between my feet which I was able to put out by covering it with a cigarette tin, and one of the girl's hair caught fire, but otherwise we escaped unhurt. After the planes had gone I told everyone to stay still as the Japanese might return; on the 23rd they came low down and machine-gunned people on the streets. However, a few moments later there was a roaring and shouting and my husband, using the most appalling language, was demanding to know why we were not helping to put out the fires. The cook house was blazing, also the covered way and the servants' quarters. A house at the corner of the compound near the trenches got a direct hit and was burnt to nothing in twenty minutes. We lived in the same type of house, brick nogging downstairs, all teak upstairs and with a wooden shingle roof.

We eventually got breakfast at about 3 p.m., but my first action on returning home was to pack two suitcases with two of everything each of us needed, to be kept in the dugout in case our house got a direct hit.

We dined at about 9 p.m. It was a jolly good dinner eaten by candlelight and lamps as the electricity was still not functioning. We were all so tired after the various excitements of the day that the party broke up early and we all retired to much needed sleep.

Shortly after the Christmas Day raid our Burmese servants, both of whom had been with us for years, asked if we would help them financially to send their wives and children back to their villages near Mandalay. Once these women and children were away these boys told us they would be quite willing to stay in Rangoon. Our cook was an Indian and we had promised to look after him and his family.

We sent these Burmese women and children off and for some days the boys worked very well and seemed quite contented. Then on about 3rd January 1942, after we had moved house and shortly after they had been given their month's wages, they both asked permission to go down to the Bazaar to buy food. They never returned and we were told by the Indian cook that one of the wives had come back and persuaded both of them to leave Rangoon by the midday train. Many Burmese are rather like that, one rarely finds the loyalty and faithful service so typical of the old type of Indian bearer. Years later, when my husband was with the military administration on the re-occupation of Burma, he went to visit the elder of these two servants. He and his wife – the cause of all the trouble – were found at a small tea shop they had opened on the Mandalay-Maymyo road and at the sight of my husband both ran out of the shop and threw their arms in greeting round his neck, quite unrepentant at having deserted us.

Their departure made life for a while very difficult. There were six of us living and feeding in the flat above the office, and there were always two or more visitors – usually unexpected – for lunch or dinner, and I was left with only a young Burmese boy to do all the housework. Fortunately the cook found a friend, an Indian named Paul Peter, who proved one of the best servants we had ever had and who walked out to India in our party.

Shortly before New Year a crowd of European refugees arrived from Tenasserim and Mergui, mostly rubber planters, and until we could find suitable accommodation for them they were housed at one of the large hotels. I went to inspect the Japanese Consulate, which was then empty, to see if it would be suitable as a hostel for these men. It was a very fine brick house, but inside was complete chaos; the remains of a meal was still on the table – and how it smelt; mattresses were in all the rooms upstairs and down, and dust and cobwebs were over everything. We had it cleaned up and the next day took some of the refugees to the house. One of the first things they found was an opera hat belonging to a Japanese with a very small head. The antics with this hat of a very large and fat rubber planter clad in shirt and shorts kept us in fits of laughter; we had had very little to laugh at up to then.

Two of these refugees came to live with us, as the housing shortage was so acute. One of them annoyed me intensely as whenever there was a raid he would join me in the trenches and then fall fast asleep, snoring like a pig. I used to sit in those trenches longing for someone to talk to.

Early in January we moved to a Chinese house in the shadow of the Shwe Dagon Pagoda. It would be more accurate to write 'I moved', as I had to cope with everything, my husband being tied to the office. It was great good luck that there were no air raid warnings whilst the move was in progress, as the drivers of the Evacuation lorries which we were using had a habit of dashing out of town as hard as they could as soon as they heard the sirens, and were sometimes not seen again for twenty-four hours or more.

The Evacuation Department was given the job of requisitioning all houses in Rangoon required by the Army, Navy, or Civil Government, and it was part of my duty to go and inspect the principal buildings and see for what they might be suitable. There was rather an interesting sequel to this. Over three years later when I was in Calcutta I was bidden to Fort William and in very strict secrecy asked to describe most of the main buildings on a very large-scale map of Rangoon. This was the Headquarters of the planners for the recapture of that town by a landing from the sea.

In the Chinese house to which we had moved the office telephone at night was switched through to our upstairs flat. Night after night, clad in pyjamas and dressing gown and with a book to while away the time, I would sit at this telephone to await any crisis or new excitement. When that occurred I would try and find my husband, who was then usually out all night loading up boats with refugees. I would telephone to the Race Course camp, or failing to catch him there, ring up the Silver Grill, to where I knew he and his officers used to dash for a drink at odd times during the night, particularly if there was an 'Alert' on. At times when he could not be found I had to do the best I could, which was not always easy as, for example, the night the Commandant of the Palace camp got so drunk, which has been related in an earlier chapter.

On the occasion when a boat was allocated to Anglo-Indian and Anglo-Burman refugees it was announced that tickets would be sold at evacuation Headquarters on a definite day. This was not strictly correct, as tickets were distributed to Agents for sale by them. Resulting from this error the office was besieged by nearly a thousand men and women of all races demanding tickets. The Director was out, as also were most of his officers. We had retained about two hundred and fifty tickets in the office for issue to wives and families of the Rangoon Town Police, and the sale of these excited the crowds outside, who refused to believe there were no more available. Eventually they became very threatening and unpleasant and I was obliged to ring up the Police and ask for a detachment to be sent round to clear the office. As at the time there were only girls in the office, the experience had for a while been decidedly frightening.

Though all of us were working all day from the very early hours until very late at night, we seldom could get a good night's rest, mainly owing to the frequent air raid alarms. We got so fed up with constantly going into the trenches only to find the raid was fourteen miles away at Mingaladon, that my husband and I decided one night that we would take no notice of the sirens. This was just after we had occupied the trenches five times one night. However, just after we got to sleep the alarm sounded; the dogs who slept in our bedroom made for the door, but we managed to pacify them. Then suddenly there was the most terrific roar which shot us out of our beds, the dogs yapping and frantically scratching at the door. We made for the trenches as hard as we could only then to realise that it was a new heavy anti-aircraft battery which that day must have taken up a position close to our house. After that it was never any use trying to sleep during a raid. Once the 'all clear' sounded the dogs would immediately leave the trench and make for their baskets.

Life settled down into a routine until the fall of Singapore on 15th February 1942. A day or two after a friend of ours in a big shipping firm rang me up and asked if there were any boxes I would like to send to India. I had four packed ready, two small ones containing old family silver and two trunks containing our warm clothes, a collection of ivory and various odd valuables. It appeared that the Captain of the boat would take these boxes over as his own personal property if I delivered them to the boat, which I did. Months later, after we had arrived in Calcutta, we found them in a store waiting to be claimed. We were amongst the lucky ones who were able to save a few of our possessions. I had packed these boxes in a great hurry on moving into the Chinese house. How hurried can be realised when on unpacking the contents in Calcutta I discovered the large dust cover containing my fur coat was empty.

At about this time the lady in charge of the Forces Canteen had asked me to attend regularly if possible, as so many volunteer helpers were leaving Rangoon, often without any warning, that at times she had only one or two helpers at night. I, therefore, endeavoured to go every night if I could be spared from Evacuation Headquarters. On the 17th there were only three of us there and at 8 p.m. I asked one of the troops if there had been anything interesting on the wireless news. He replied with the startling news that the Japanese were only about fifty miles from Rangoon; this meant Pegu, on the main Mandalay railway and road, thus cutting off any direct communication with the north. I nearly dropped the tray of bacon and eggs I was carrying, the news was so alarming; and was very surprised on returning to Evacuation Headquarters at about midnight to find no signs of packing up. My husband got such a shock when I repeated to him the news that he at once rang up the station to book seats on the Mandalay mail train the next day for all the female staff. The mail train was full so we were booked on the slow train due to leave at 10.30 a.m. The news proved to be not quite correct, the Japanese being fifty miles from Pegu, but it was just as well my husband did not know this as their subsequent advance was very rapid and a few days later we might not have got any seats at all.

I spent most of the remainder of the night packing and we left the house at 9.30 a.m. No sooner had we arrived at the station than the sirens went and everyone disappeared. Fortunately we were cheered up by the arrival of Booth Russell with a large bag of chocolates which we all ate sitting on our bags. Theft was so rampant that we dared not leave our possessions.

The train eventually left about midday and it certainly was a slow one. We hoped to get some tea at the Railway Refreshment Room at Pegu, but it had been taken over by the Army that morning. At about 9 p.m. we arrived at Kyauktaga and collected all the small children of the Bishop Strachan's Home who had been sent from Rangoon. Kyauktaga was no longer safe and my husband had arranged for their accommodation at Mogok north of Mandalay. We had twelve small kids in our carriage and they were all extremely good. On arrival at Toungoo about midnight we found about twenty girls and a mistress from one of the Moulmein schools, who had been sent to Thandaung the local hill station of Toungoo, and were also being moved farther north. At Toungoo the two officers my husband had sent with us left the train. They thought we were safe from bombing attacks and other troubles and the train continued its journey at about 2 a.m.

We arrived at Pyinmana at about 10.30 a.m. and there had a large breakfast at the Railway Refreshment Rooms, the first real food we had had since leaving Rangoon. I ate mine very quickly, fed the two dogs and then gave them a walk along the platform. I was at the far end when I heard the sound of planes, and, having been in all the raids in Rangoon, recognised them as Japanese. They made a distinctive noise, it sounded like a motor engine missing on one cylinder. I spoke to one of the women in a carriage near me and as we were wondering what to do the first bomb fell in the station yard. I waited for no more, jumped down on the rails between the carriage wheels and the platform, shoved the dogs under the carriage and tried to get there myself, but found too many bits and pieces in the way. All I could do was to lie flat on my tummy on, incidentally, a bag of 5,000 rupees my husband had given me for general expenses. One of the American missionaries was in front of me and after the first wave passed over she started to get up. I yelled to her to lie still as I felt there would be others, which there were, two more, and then the planes flew off. Whilst the raid lasted the noise was terrific, incendiaries and anti-personnel bombs seemingly in hundreds; the latter are small and make little impression on the ground but burst outwards; provided one is below ground level they are not very destructive.

Miss E. and I staggered on to the platform, both absolutely filthy, and after tying my dogs to the fence I went to see what had happened. The next carriage to where I had been lying had had a direct hit killing outright one of the staff's grandmother and injuring three others on the staff who had been lying on the floor. Several other carriages were smashed and in flames, and I found the Headmistress of the Moulmein school badly hurt; she died that evening. Mrs. Munroe, my husband's stenographer, had also been severely wounded and died two days later. I walked along to the Refreshment Room to get some water for Mrs. Munroe and was quite unmoved by the terrible sights I encountered. Normally I should have been violently sick, but I suppose I was still shocked and dazed by the terrible noise of the raid, the planes had come so very low. I found that a bomb had fallen on either side of the Refreshment Room, which was a sea of glass, and a lot of the girls of the staff, caught inside, had taken refuge under the tables and so were unhurt. I managed to find some drinking water and returned to see what could be done for the wounded. Altogether seven members of my party, which included numerous relations of the staff, were wounded. Six of them died in the Pyinmana Hospital through lack of proper attention, though no blame can be attached to the doctor and nurses.

The raid had not been confined to the station; large fires were blazing all over the town and the casualties must have been very numerous. The Pyinmana Hospital is quite small with a very limited staff, and they must have had at least two hundred wounded from the train alone, apart from the hundreds in the town.

Very fortunately the last carriage containing the school children was untouched, so all of them escaped unhurt.

Just then two officers who were passing through the town in their jeep came on to the platform and offered to help. I got them to take Mrs. Munroe and the other badly wounded woman to the hospital at once. These men returned very shortly with two lorries they had stopped, and these did excellent work taking the wounded to the hospital and the dead to the cemetery just outside the town. I sent all the school children to a big American Agricultural College in the town. The students had been sent home and the Principal, Rev. Case, whom I knew having lived in Pyinmana before the war, was most kind and helpful, put all the houses at our disposal and fed us from the produce of his marvelous garden. Whilst we were still trying to collect all our belongings from the railway carriages, Mr. Smith, a Conservator of Forests, arrived with a lot of students from the Pyinmana Forest School and they were most helpful in getting our possessions to the Agricultural College.

On arrival there I discovered I had damaged my knees quite badly jumping down on to the railway line and landing on all fours on the flinty metal. They were also black with dirt. I cleaned them up as best as I could, stuck some plaster on, and the next day walked up to the Civil Station to see if I could find the sub-Divisional Officer or Mr. Smith and make arrangements for getting away from Pyinmana. The evacuation of Rangoon had been ordered by then so all trains passing through were packed with people. Everyone was down cleaning up the town and putting out the fires, so finding no one who could be of any help I telephoned to Mandalay and asked the Commissioner to send down an ambulance to remove the wounded, as the Pyinmana Hospital was crowded out.

I managed to get all the school children off by train that afternoon and the ambulance arrived next morning. By then all my wounded had died, so the ambulance was packed with elderly people and mothers with children. That left about a dozen of us and we were preparing to go out on the road and lorry hop when two ancient Burmese buses arrived from Mr. Smith to take us on our way north. We all piled in, including the two dogs, put most of the luggage on the roof, and started off. We chugged along, having to stop every ten miles or so to fill up the radiator with water as the engine was constantly boiling.

We arrived at Yamethin where much to our joy we were met by Mr. Booth Russell in a borrowed jeep. He had been sent up by my husband as soon as they had heard in Rangoon that our train had been bombed. He took us to an American, a Colonel Vaughan. He was dealing with 'Lease Lend' material for

China, loading it up in lorries and sending it via the Burma-China road. The Colonel was awfully good to us, gave us some much needed food and drink and lent us two Chinese lorries with American drivers, into which I put everyone and all the baggage. Mrs. Pughe, I and the two dogs went in Booth Russell's jeep.

We eventually arrived in Mandalay at about 7 p.m., I looking the complete refugee in filthy shorts, coloured shirt and with the plaster on my knees flapping in the breeze. We went straight to the Commissioner's house and he very kindly invited Mrs. Pughe and me to stay with him in his already almost full house. I was lucky to find a Civil Surgeon Colonel living with him, as this doctor cleaned up my knees properly and gave me the most enormous shot of anti-tetanus, which gave me a very poor night's sleep, my arm was so painful.

Next day, wishing to be of some use to my host, I volunteered to do anything that was required. He asked me to become his telephone girl and sort of personal assistant. This entailed interviewing various callers when he was out, taking down hundreds of telephone messages, and also sending out many more, as he always left me with a long list when he went out. I felt very important as I used to say: "This is a priority call, Commissioner of Mandalay speaking", and then would possibly order thousands of gallons of octane from Yenangyaung to be sent to various places all over the country. Some of the messages were most interesting.

Meanwhile every day and at all times people were arriving in dozens from Rangoon. They all came to the Commissioner's house to find out about accommodation. A lot went up to Maymyo, the hill station forty miles away, and we found room for the rest of the thirteen bankers who had left Rangoon by special train with an air escort. Only one had a wife with him and she only stayed in Mandalay for a short time, eventually flying to India from Shwebo.

After the air raid on 3rd April 1942 (Good Friday) when large parts of the main streets of Mandalay were either blasted or destroyed by fire these bankers left for India, only the Reserve bank carrying on till the latter part of April at Shwebo.

I anxiously asked all the arrivals from Rangoon for news of my husband, and though most of them were able to tell me something I found out later that a lot of these bits were very inaccurate. On the Friday afternoon the Inspector General of Civil Hospitals' bag and baggage arrived in two ambulances complete with Frigidaire and quite a lot of other household furniture. The drivers were sent to the house which had been taken for him and the great man himself arrived shortly after with five nurses from the Rangoon hospitals. The Commissioner was away, and I had just finished giving them much needed drinks and they had departed to their residence when my husband walked in much to my surprise, as the last news I had heard was that he was still in Rangoon.

CHAPTER IV

On the afternoon of the 24th February several of us visited Thonze and, ten miles beyond, Tharrawaddy. Both towns were packed with refugees; at Tharrawaddy it was almost impossible to get near the station for the crowds waiting for trains to Prome.

The Civil Authorities, particularly the medical staff, were being worked off their feet. One of the trains from Rangoon had picked up hundreds more refugees en route who, in typically Eastern fashion, climbed on to the roofs of the carriages or hung like limpets to the outside of the doors. A narrow and low bridge had swept off scores of these passengers, all of whom were either killed or very seriously injured.

Our services were not required, so after another night's rest we drove on to Prome, about ninety miles distant. Prome was full of memories for me as I had been stationed there as a bachelor in 1923-24 and returned as a married man in1928-29. Situated on the Irrawaddy river, it was the terminus of the railway from Rangoon, and was also a port of call for all river boats to and from Mandalay. The large mail and cargo boats arriving from Rangoon stayed the night in Prome before proceeding up the river. There were also smaller boats running a local service calling at all the smaller river towns. These smaller boats were now being used to take to Mandalay the thousands of refugees arriving by train.

The congestion was appalling, the riverside being blocked with men and women waiting for the boats. They were still expected to pay their fares and many, being penniless, were waiting at the riverside in the hope of 'jumping' a ship. Being only the Director of Evacuation for Rangoon I had no authority in the District, but with the 87,000 rupees I had brought with me from Rangoon I was able to charter two boats and have them loaded up without the delay of selling tickets. It was some time later that I heard the Army, before Rangoon was evacuated, had taken over the whole of the Flotilla Company's fleet, and therefore, no fares should rightly have been demanded. I have often wondered what happened to the 15,000 rupees I paid out for those two boats.

On one of these ships I placed a European named Hamilton in charge of the passengers. I had first met him in Rangoon, arriving at my office on 22nd February, very worried and harassed. He had in his peace-time capacity as stevedore been working for either the Army or Navy, and had been guaranteed a passage to India for his wife and three daughters if he stayed till the last, but that afternoon he had been told no boat was available and was advised to find his way up country. I was able to put him on a train to Tharrawaddy and on the 24th had got him on a further stage of the journey. His daughters were very charming girls, ranging in ages from about fifteen to nineteen, and the thought of them being left to the 'mercy' of the Japanese was unthinkable. Later chapters will relate how this family failed to escape from Burma yet had a miraculous escape for nearly three years from any contact with the enemy.

The Civil Authorities in Prome were still trying to cope with the crowds making for Taungup, necessitating constant control of the movement of refugees across the river. Records show that on the 23rd and 24th of February fourteen thousand arrived at Taungup and from that date till the end of March at least one thousand five hundred a day completed the journey.

By the time we arrived in Prome the cholera epidemic was under control though by no means

An Irrawaddy Flotilla Express steamer licensed to carry 40 first and second class
and many hundred deck passengers: the 250 ft. 'flat' lashed on each side
could carry up to 2,000 tons of cargo.

stamped out, and those in authority were a very harassed crowd of officials. With the evacuation of Rangoon their staff had been augmented and our help was not required.

Owing to the crowds and the threat of cholera we had camped in a Forest Reserve about ten miles north of the town, and on the morning of the 26th we left this pleasant spot to drive north to Taungdwingyi, where we arrived that evening. This was a sub-Divisional Headquarters of Magwe District and the Headquarters of the Divisional Forest Officer. I had been stationed there in 1924-25 and had very pleasant memories of some magnificent shooting during that period. The forests were full of elephants, tsaing (wild cow) and bison. Just before I had left in 1925 an officer of the Geological Survey, who always refused to carry a rifle in the jungle, had been killed by an old bull bison he met in a narrow stream bed.

As we drove into the Rest House compound on the 26th evening we found it already occupied by a Burmese Police Officer and his English wife. This officer had in Rangoon been organizing a band of guerillas to stay behind should Rangoon fall; his presence in Taungdwingyi was therefore rather surprising.

I was in rather a quandary, as having been working in Rangoon more or less independently I had no Departmental Head to whom to apply for instructions, and did not know where we could be of most use. Further, I had no authority outside Rangoon. I knew Government was setting up the Secretariat in Maymyo, the hill station about forty miles northeast of Mandalay, so decided I should find out there if I and my staff were still required. It seemed pointless at this stage to take all my transport with me, it was at least two hundred miles further north and we might be required to operate in Lower Burma, so leaving the vehicles and staff at Taungdwingyi I went on alone to Mandalay.

From Taungdwingyi the road skirts Mount Popa, an extinct volcano on the edge of which reside a sect of Burmese who have the power of taming, or more correctly hypnotizing, hamadryads, the king cobra whose bite is fatal. These snakes are usually to be found in pairs and there is a firm belief that if one of a pair is killed the mate will always reap vengeance on the killer. They are one of the few snakes, if not the only kind, which will follow a human, and they can travel as fast as a galloping horse. I have never visited this sect at Mount Popa, but have seen photos of the female members kissing the snakes on the mouth as the reptiles in typical cobra manner erect their heads.

The drive to Mandalay, except for appalling roads, was uneventful, and I arrived the same evening.

The Commissioner of Mandalay was an old friend of mine, having been Deputy Commissioner in Toungoo when I was stationed there in 1939-40. He was known throughout Burma as 'Matthew John' or 'M.J.', so knowing I should get the latest news from him I drove up to his house to have the very pleasant surprise of finding my wife on the doorstep. She, it appeared, was doorkeeper, secretary, telephone girl and general stooge for 'M.J.', though still only able to hobble about, having both knees bandaged and plastered as the result of her contact with the rail metal at Pyinmana when she hid under the carriage during the bombing of her train.

M.J. gave me a warm welcome, also an excellent dinner, and my wife and I sat talking well on into the night relating to each other our experiences. I then for the first time heard the details of the tragedy at Pyinmana and of the death of my efficient and charming stenographer, Mrs. Munroe. This lady had been offered a lift from Rangoon to Mandalay in a friend's car, but had considered it her duty to go by train with the rest of the staff, only to be mortally wounded by an exploding bomb as she was attempting to get out of the train. Another casualty, fortunately not fatal, was a grand Anglo-Indian girl who was taken to Mandalay Hospital. This girl had a remarkable escape later on when the Mandalay Hospital was bombed. A few seconds after she left her room to go to her mother who was a housekeeper, a bomb crashed through the ceiling of her room and exploded.

Despite her lameness my wife, I gathered, was kept very busy as M.J., like most officials up country, was completely in the dark as to what was happening. His patience and good temper, never very noticeable characteristics, had been tried very highly by a constant stream of visitors asking, and expecting, the impossible. On one occasion he had escaped to his bathroom leaving my wife to cope with a party of hysterical females; on another she had had to placate a crowd of thirteen very irate bankers who had arrived from Rangoon, M.J. at the sight of them having disappeared in his car to Maymyo.

So far Mandalay had not had to tackle any serious refugee problem. Two temporary camps had been constructed capable of accommodating about eight thousand, and a third small camp for Muslims had been formed near a village where Muslims predominated. All three camps, which were then not even half full, had been placed under the charge of an Indo-Burman Additional Deputy Commissioner who appeared to be dealing with the situation satisfactorily and whose dignity would be most hurt if I were placed in control.

The military authorities, however, were making heavy demands for civil labour, and the Commissioner suggested that my staff deal with all labour control, for which work in Rangoon I had recruited a special staff.

At this time the Mandalay Fort had been taken over by the Army and was being used as a main depot. This fort was a most historic monument dating back to the time when Mandalay was the old capital of Burma prior to the British occupation. It then contained the King's Palace and the houses of his entourage, but under British rule had become a military cantonment containing barracks and officers' houses. The fort was formed by four enormous walls, each one and a quarter miles long and surrounded by a moat. This moat was crossed by four road bridges, one in the centre of each wall, the entrances being closed by massive gates. Outside each gate there were two very thick tall teak posts under each of which, history relates, workmen were buried alive in the construction of the Fort so that their spirits would always be on guard.

King Thibaw, who was captured by the British in the Palace in 1885, was one of the last Eastern despots whose absolute rule over his subjects is very largely a history of murder and tyranny. There is a walled enclosure behind the Palace building to which this old tyrant is said to have invited one day all his male relations who might have aspirations to the throne. He then let loose within the four walls his herd of elephants to trample to death every one of these possible usurpers.

The Palace, burnt down during the recapture of Mandalay in 1945, was made almost entirely of teak, with enormous teak pillars in the Throne Room gaudily encrusted with millions of small pieces of coloured glass. The whole edifice was a tawdry affair. For some time after the second Burmese war the Palace was used as a European Club until Lord Curzon, then Viceroy of India, ordered it to be maintained as a historical monument. A new Club had been built nearby, and when I arrived at the end of February this was the only building destroyed in the single bombing raid the town had experienced up till then. The members' main concern, however, was over the complete destruction of the very large stocks of whiskey.

The military depot surrounded the Palace and was connected with the main Mandalay-Rangoon railway by a line which crossed the moat at the south-west corner. Hundreds of tons of every type of military stores were being dealt with at this depot requiring the employment of nearly one thousand civil labourers daily. Other labour was needed outside the Fort for the construction of aerodromes, and for the stocking of the more dangerous supplies in widely-spaced stores in the surrounding countryside.

The civil station, that is, the residence of most of the Government officials, was situated on the moat road east of the Fort. On the south side most of the residences of the commercial firms lined the moat road, behind which were the Police lines and one or two large schools. South of these was a large Anglo-Burman and Anglo-Indian residential area in which most of the houses were made of wood.

The main shopping centre, bazaar and Burmese quarter lay between the west side of the Fort and the Irrawaddy. Mandalay hill, capped by a mass of pagodas and priest's quarters, lay to the north of the Fort. Unlike Rangoon, the population was predominantly Burmese, a large proportion of whom cultivated the vast surrounding area of rice fields.

Having sent for my staff and transport my next task was to find accommodation. My wife had housed all the survivors from the Pyinmana raid in the American Baptist Mission School southeast of the town, and the Headmistress was agreeable to their remaining there.

For ourselves, we were invited to share a house which had been requisitioned by a very old friend of ours who was Chief Censor of Burma. He was an ex Indian cavalry officer who transferred to the Burma Military Police and had retired several years before. When the Japanese declared war he was recalled and on arriving in Burma, being then nearing sixty years of age, was appointed Chief Censor. His wife joined him later and those two, Tommy and Nancy as they are known to their many hundreds of friends, gave us a very warm welcome. He was one of the old school so regrettably rare these days, apparently treating everything as a joke and again, apparently, never over-exerting himself yet actually the most efficient, hardworking and thorough disciplinarian one could meet anywhere. In the days that were to come with the temperature at around 110 degrees, often with no electric light or fans and after a day of bombing raids and fires, Tommy would turn up to dinner immaculate in white shirt, black evening trousers, complete with collar and black tie, and was never ruffled. If there was any rescue work to be done, out he would come still in his evening kit, only too ready to help and thoroughly enjoying a new experience. I had heard it said that many years before at a party at the Rangoon Boat Club he had livened up the proceedings by diving off the Club verandah into the Royal Lakes clothed in his tails, white waistcoat and all. I can quite believe it.

There will be several references in subsequent chapters to Tommy and Nancy, but those references will never describe adequately nor, I think, will those two ever realise how their courage, understanding and cheerfulness inspired all of us on the staff of the Evacuation Department.

Almost opposite their house I was very fortunate in being able to requisition the Wesley Girls High School, a very fine brick building which would serve as my office and house most of the staff. Nearby there was a large building with an extensive garden which was admirably suited for a transport park.

The convoy took several days on the journey from Taungdwingyi, having experienced considerable difficulty with the unwieldy Rangoon Electric Tramway Company's buses over the very narrow and rough-surfaced roads round Mount Popa. However, not one vehicle had been lost, thanks to Green's foresight in Rangoon. Petrol dumps, supposedly laid down specially for motorists leaving Rangoon, had repeatedly failed us, and but for our own stocks of petrol and diesel oil we should never have reached Mandalay. The Officer at one dump, interpreting his instructions as to apply only to private cars, had refused to supply our lorries. Whilst two of my officers kept him in animated argument, half a dozen others crept into the back of the dump and carried off a forty-gallon drum – thoroughly illegal and undisciplined, but decidedly enterprising. They were all non-officials and loathed red tape.

Shortly after arriving in Mandalay, we heard that the Japanese had delayed entering Rangoon, and, not knowing about a road block on the Prome road, it seemed possible to get back there with a fleet of lorries and rescue much needed stocks of equipment and food supplies. After some discussion, Walter Voehringher and I decided to return with several European members of Messrs. Steel Brothers. Arrangements were all complete, lorries overhauled and got ready, and Walter and I arrived one morning early at Steel's office in Mandalay to pick up the other members of the party. We then heard that news had come through less than an hour before that the Japanese had occupied the town.

We only took a day to settle in at Mandalay and then got down to dealing with the civil labour problem. Burmese labour almost immediately proved very unreliable and very difficult to control. They had no idea of punctuality and would arrive at all hours of the morning; one could never guarantee any definite number arriving each day and they were very apt to get fed up with the work before the day's task was completed, and would quietly disappear. They would, however, always turn up at the end of the day for their wages. At this time the Army would collect the men in military lorries, would supervise the work and would return them to our office in the evening to be paid out. All labour demanded their pay at the end of each day's work, which meant payment in coin and not notes. Every evening the Army officers would complain that only half the number required had been on the job, though invariably the full number would get off those lorries.

We decided to replace this Burmese labour with Indian refugee labour, necessitating loading and unloading the lorries morning and evening at the refugee camps. I then paid my first visit to these camps and was horrified at the conditions. One large camp had no latrines whatsoever and only a few had huts. Most of the refugees were living under the shade of the trees, two or three thousand of them huddled together in a very limited space. The camp stank and, with the water supply very far from satisfactory, an epidemic was certain before long. The second camp contained about three thousand occupants and had sufficient latrines for only about one hundred. An excellent Indian schoolmaster and his wife were in charge and were doing their best, but both complained bitterly to me of their difficulties.

The food supplied to these refugees was of the poorest quality, much of the rice being almost inedible. The Muslims were better off as they were being fed by the Headman of the village, but I was staggered to hear the price he was charging per head.

Unfortunately I had no authority to interfere, and could only warn M.J. that there would be very serious trouble if conditions did not improve and if there was any large increase in the numbers of refugees arriving in Mandalay. Already a trickle had started to appear from Lower Burma.

The able-bodied occupants of the camps were only too ready to earn some money and we had no difficulty in obtaining the full labour force we required. We dispensed with Army transport and used our own vehicles, also keeping staff with the labour during the day. Each labourer as he got into the lorry in the morning was issued with a ticket; this was taken away when he started work and was re-issued to him as he was collected from the work, ensuring that only those who worked got paid. Even so, they were up to every trick and were as slippery customers as the Burmans, though far better workers.

During this period when life was comparatively quiet I was able to improve the quality of my staff by the recruitment of several new arrivals from Rangoon. One of these men, Condie by name, had had a very lucky escape. He had been a Corporation engineer at the Rangoon water works and, when all his Indian staff bolted, carried on alone keeping the furnaces going and the pumps working till almost the very last day before the Japanese entered the town. He had then got on a train, the last train out of Rangoon run specially for a few last ditchers, which after covering about thirty miles came under machine gun fire. Unknown to the Army, the Japanese coming down the Mandalay road to Rangoon had branched off to the west and formed a road block on the Rangoon-Prome road. The train stopped and Condie made for the forest beside the railway line and then had a hair-raising three or four days making his way northwards to Thonze through the enemy's patrols.

This road block was nearly far more successful than the Japanese could possibly have anticipated, as it held up the remains of our Army retreating from Pegu, with whom were the whole of our Army Headquarters including General Alexander, General Hutton, and several other high-ranking officers. During this hold-up when the Army was being attacked from the East, a large force of Japanese moved round behind the road block and southwards towards Rangoon skirting the western side of our perimeter, I believe less than a mile away. Fortunately, neither they nor our troops realised the two forces were in such close proximity. It was only after almost half a British Infantry Battalion had been wiped out that some tanks of the Armoured Brigade managed to break through the road block, enabling our Army with Headquarters to escape.

We were also assisted during this period by a 'Friends' Ambulance Unit. This unit had come out to Burma to work mainly with the Chinese, but had been hampered by lack of transport. The day after evacuation of Rangoon was ordered several of these very tough lads had gone down to the Rangoon docks and, finding crates containing all the necessary parts, had with their own hands assembled two complete lorry chassis and, using parts of the crates as seats, had driven these vehicles the four hundred and fifty odd miles to Mandalay.

Daily now more refugees were arriving, a hundred or so to start with, soon increasing to a thousand or more. Many, taking one look at the camps, would move elsewhere seeking good shade and water, a favourite site being the wooded east bank of the Irrawaddy.

There was an additional reason for the selection of this bank. The only known route to India started from Monywa and went via Kalewa and Tamu to Imphal in Assam. This path was now in process of conversion by the Army to form their main supply route from India to Burma, in fact their only supply route now that Rangoon had fallen. To prevent the labourers on this road being alarmed and deserting as the result of harassing tales from refugees, and also to prevent the spread of any epidemic, the Army had endeavoured to stop any movement of refugees west of the Irrawaddy until construction had been completed. I did not realise then that, in anticipation of a large refugee population moving along this road, the Army were taking steps to lay down food supplies at the main villages. The river was constantly patrolled and a barbed wire barrier with an armed guard was eventually placed across the Ava bridge, the one and only bridge connecting Mandalay with the west bank.

By camping on the east bank, refugees hoped to be able to slip across at night. Many others with the same idea in their minds camped in empty trucks at any railway siding between Mandalay and the bridge.

In spite of these additional settlements the camps soon became overflowing, and by the 21st March it was estimated that over thirty thousand refugees were in or around Mandalay. Cholera had broken out. It was first reported by my labour staff and I passed on the news to the Commissioner, who then asked me to take over full control. The Public Health Department in Mandalay had at this time no European staff and the senior officers were all Burmese. They may have been responsible for these camps; I do know that none of my staff ever once saw an officer of that Department at any of them. Had proper sanitation been carried out and the camps been visited frequently by sanitary inspectors and health officers, this epidemic would never have occurred.

On the afternoon of the 21st, accompanied by Booth Russell, I drove round each of these three camps and also visited some of the squatters. The conditions we found were too disgusting and unbelievable to report. Booth Russell, tough as he was, was physically sick over the side of the jeep, and I was not far from that stage. In addition to cholera, smallpox was also raging, and the dead, some very dead, and the dying were everywhere. With typical Eastern fatalism the refugees appeared to have resigned themselves to the inevitable: death. They made no effort to improve conditions or even bury their own dead.

On returning to our Headquarters all the officers were called up, and that evening and well on into the night we decided on the re-organisation of the Department in preparation for what turned out to be seven weeks of filth, sweat, heat and never-ending toil.

CHAPTER V

By the morning of 22nd March 1942, the department was re-organised into the following sections: - transport remained under Green, labour control under Andrewartha assisted by Bob Forrest, burial squads each under a separate officer and each squad had its own transport, supplies were under the control of Rev. Crane, camp construction and movement of refugees under Ricketts with Booth Russell and Voehringher on roving commissions which included the collection of money from Shwebo. I had no medical staff.

The burial squads with their transport started off at dawn, searching each camp and every area where refugees might be squatting. Early in the day I received a request from them for paraffin as some of the bodies were too decomposed to move and had to be burnt in situ. When they returned that evening, approximately eight hundred bodies had been dealt with. Daily for the next three weeks, at the end of which period the epidemic was under control, that section was fully employed and had burnt or buried over five thousand corpses. The dead were everywhere and no one had made any attempt to remove them. One was found on the iron bridge over the railway at the main station; he had been there for several days. In one squatters' camp discovered near the river bank there were more corpses than living. Wagons on railway sidings were full of the dead.

These squads from the first experienced difficulty in obtaining labour for this most gruesome task. The Burmese villagers would not look at the job and even the offer of double rates of pay could not attract the Indian refugee. Finally these extra rates with a generous tot of native spirit before and after the day's work were accepted, but the staff did not realise, that, due to under-nourishment, this labour was not capable of standing the normal dose of native liquor. On the first occasion the coolies became so hilarious and unsteady that many fell into the graves as they threw in the corpses. Amongst themselves this was considered a huge joke, but the ration was thereafter reduced. Each night the lorries used by them had to be thoroughly disinfected.

My burial staff were supposed not to deal with the Mandalay Civil station, which was under the control of the local Health Department. However, one morning we left our house to find a corpse at the gate and, as repeated requests for its removal to the Health authorities produced no results, we thereafter covered the whole town in our search for bodies.

The two original camps had become plague spots necessitating the immediate removal of all the occupants and the destruction by fire of all the buildings. There was no time to construct new camps. Providentially it was the dry season and we were able to shift everyone round the large lake at Tagundaing, south of the city, where the refugees were told to squat until new camps could be prepared.

About this time, a grey-haired couple entered my office and offered their services. The husband, in what sounded like broad American, complained bitterly that they had been sent out of Rangoon as being too old, but that they were both tough and were prepared to do anything and go anywhere, only stipulating that if employed they were allowed to stay to the end and not be sent away as soon as there was any danger. They were a Dr. and Mrs. Jury; he had been the Canadian Head of the Judson College at the Rangoon University; both he and his wife were well over sixty years of age, and from that day till we

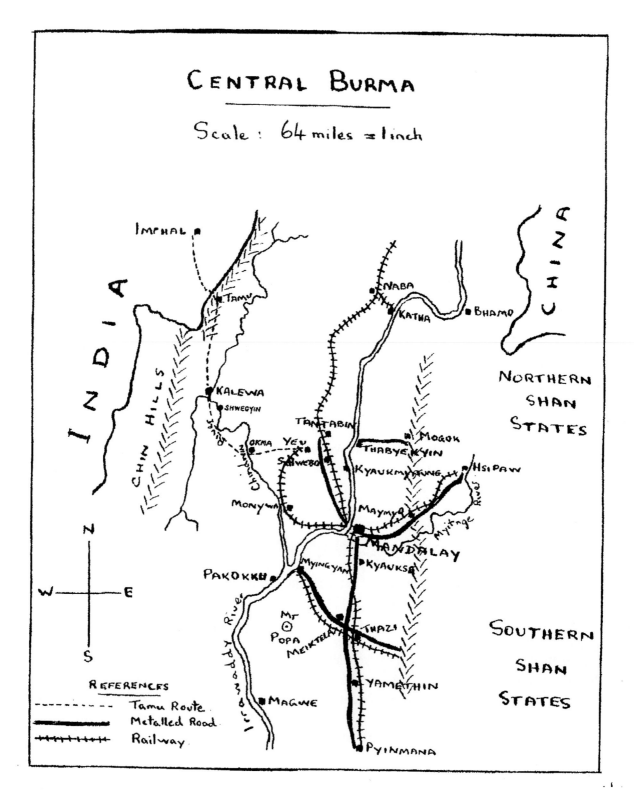

Map of Central Burma

landed at Imphal about eleven weeks later that grand old couple never spared themselves, set a never to be forgotten example to all of us and worked wonders. I was very gratified when the Doctor was awarded the M.B.E. for his services; hundreds, probably thousands, of women and children have to thank that grand old couple for being alive today.

Another arrival offering his services was a tough old gentleman named Williams. Except that he was a refugee from Tenasserim his past was somewhat of a mystery; he was obviously down and out.

He was old and, possibly, I appeared hesitant at employing him as he interrupted to remark: "Don't worry about my age or my looks. I have no ties, no family, and it does not matter what happens to me, but I can work and I will tackle anything." I took a chance and gave him the job of getting a new camp constructed as quickly a possible. He worked like a slave, living on the site and refusing to return at night to Mandalay. Before his camp was half finished he had collected and housed several hundred of the refugees, but through carelessness contracted cholera, died and was buried in the Mandalay cemetery. We had no knowledge of his next of kin, but if any of them read this book they will know that Williams gave his life helping others, working for them from dawn to dusk and never thinking of his own comfort or health. For him as for many others during this evacuation 'the trumpets sounded on the other side'.

The camp construction section searched the surrounding country for suitable camp sites containing good shade and an adequate water supply, and got to work erecting on the selected sites temporary huts of bamboo and thatch. Nine camps capable of accommodating about fifty thousand were selected and fit for occupation in an incredibly short time. They were not complete by any means, but each one had adequate latrines, a dispensary and store and head cover for the occupants. Construction continued after the refugees were moved in.

It was very necessary to stop indiscriminate squatting and for the Department to have authority to remove squatters to our recognised camps. This was accomplished by an order issued by the Deputy Commissioner, Mandalay, prohibiting squatting and ordering refugees to reside in Evacuation camps. To put that rule into effect was not easy, as not only did the squatters object but there were thousands of them, and all with their belongings had to be moved in our lorries. As soon as one area was cleared new arrivals would form new settlements, requiring daily inspections of all the favoured sites. We never succeeded in getting everyone into our camps, staff and transport were inadequate, but the vast majority were got under our control.

It had been difficult to persuade the squatters to stay round the Tagundaing lake, but this was accomplished by installing food issue depots at convenient points, from which the refugees could collect their rations daily. This brings me to the Supply section of the Department.

As head of this section I was most fortunate in being able to recruit the Rev. Crane, who had been in charge of the American Baptist Mission Press in Rangoon. If Crane's hustle is typical of the average American Baptist missionary, I am surprised there is a heathen left in the world. From the start we had to feed about thirty thousand, which number eventually rose to ninety thousand in Mandalay alone, with later thirty thousand or more on the west bank of the river, yet never once was there a shortage of food. We took over a rice mill, a vegetable oil mill, we requisitioned a cinema to use as a rice store, and Crane's staff searched the countryside for miles around purchasing foodstuffs.

I cannot remember the diet now, but it included rice, dried lentils, gram, potatoes, onions, cooking oil, chillies and any kind of green vegetable we could procure. Shortly after we took over, the main bazaars in Mandalay closed down, which considerably increased our difficulties. The Supply section was also responsible for finding lime, bamboos, thatch, disinfectants, paraffin, in fact everything we needed except medical stores.

Food for those thousands was a very real problem, and, to start with, we were up against a certain amount of antagonism from the leading Burmese contractors. One or two of these men, under the arrangements with the Additional Deputy Commissioner before our arrival, had been coining money supplying at top prices the cheapest foodstuffs, which were frequently decayed and almost inedible. When their contracts were cancelled they tried to boycott us. The only alternative was to deal with petty traders in the surrounding villages, increasing our transport difficulties.

Distribution of the daily rations in camps was another long and finnicky task. Each individual or the head of each family had to be given his daily quota as every one of them was out to get more than he was entitled to. Each camp had to be provided with special staff for this work.

In the latter part of March the Commissioner commandeered all useful supplies including all tinned stores in the shops, the owners of many of which had left. These stores were placed in a separate house in charge of a specially appointed officer. Shortly after, we were given the tip from one of our Army friends that the military authorities intended taking over all these supplies the next day. Getting M.J.'s agreement, I mobilized my transport that night and every ounce of those stores was moved to School Hall in my Headquarters. This Hall already contained hundreds of bags of rice. These we stacked to form a series of large caves in which we packed all the additional supplies, closing the opening with more sacks of rice. By the morning there was not a sign of any of these requisitioned stores.

These stores included the remaining stocks in Mandalay of gin and sherry plus two, and only two, very precious bottles of champagne. The gin and sherry were stored in the concrete dugout in the garden of our house. The champagne was hidden, my wife receiving special instructions that it should be cherished till there was an occasion for celebration. Later, when most of the remaining European population in Mandalay, including British Army officers, came to us for extra tinned stores, one of the girls, without my wife's knowledge, sold this 'bubbly' to one of the Army officers. She was in our black books for some days after.

With all this work going on the Transport section was kept busy night and day and found it increasingly difficult to meet the constant demands for vehicles, added to which we came up against all sorts of maddening restrictions and red tape. On one occasion, the petrol control officer at Mandalay received instructions to the effect that we were not entitled to civil petrol and must obtain our requirements from the Army, or from Maymyo over forty miles away. The Army knew nothing of this and refused our demands. A journey to Maymyo only partly solved the problem, until Army Headquarters in Maymyo eventually came to the rescue. On another occasion the military authorities descended on our transport park and requisitioned all our best lorries. That again meant a journey to Maymyo, where Army Headquarters denied all knowledge of the requisitioning and gave me authority to get the vehicles back. The military requisitioning officer in Mandalay was no fool; knowing he had no proper authority he had sent the best of our vehicles off to the front immediately so that they could not be returned. In their place we were given some very ancient and decrepit Burmese buses.

However, we could not really complain as there was a battle of wits going on everywhere. In spite of this requisitioning, accidents and breakdowns, we never seemed to be short of transport, petrol, spares or tools. After seeing a broken-down Army lorry being towed into my park one night and being immediately tackled by innumerable mechanics, including two with paint pots and brushes, I thought it advisable not to enquire too deeply into the running of this most efficient section. On another occasion from a conversation I was certainly not intended to hear, I gathered that our petrol stocks were occasionally augmented by the removal at night of forty-gallon drums from the many military petrol dumps all over the countryside. It would have been useless tackling the Transport officer, Green. If one did attempt to remonstrate one was met with the most disarming air of shocked surprise that any such things could possibly be happening, followed by the excuse that with such a very mixed crowd of mechanics, none of whose records we knew, anything might happen without his, Green's, knowledge. To get the job done one had to be ruthless and permit of some elasticity in one's normal peace-time honesty.

One incident made us feel we were justified in 'acquiring' broken-down Army vehicles. We received permission to take what we needed from a park of unserviceable military lorries. There were hundreds of these vehicles and almost the first three we examined responded immediately to the self-starter after we had cleaned out a choked petrol pipe.

The labour control section was increasingly occupied as demands for thousands of labourers were received by the Army for the Shwebo-Chindwin-Tamu route, for a proposed route through the Hukong valley, for the Myitkyina-Bhamo-Shan States road and for innumerable aerodromes and depots. I had two excellent rubber planters, Andrewartha and Bob Forrest, as officers for this work, and they were joined later by a rubber planter named Bott from the Shwegyin valley. He had had an amazing experience, having failed to get across the Sittang river to join our forces near Toungoo before the Japanese surrounded his rubber estate. For days he and his Burmese wife and half-caste children hid in some natural forest in the middle of the plantation, from where he was eventually guided to the river by some of his Burmese labourers and taken across the river by canoe. Though he was well over fifty years old and had suffered considerable privation, he then acted as guide to a detachment of our forces who crossed the river to carry out a counter-attack on Shwegyin.

In carrying on with his job on my staff Bott eventually was separated from his family, but on arriving in India on foot at the end of May he immediately took steps to return to Burma, even though the Japanese were in complete occupation, in the hope of finding his wife and children. He died of, I think, malaria as he was setting out on this journey. Another man one was proud to have known.

My most important and immediate requirements were medical staff and medical supplies. Inoculation and vaccination of all the refugees had to be carried out, and at once. I was fortunate in finding an Anglo-Indian and comparatively junior District Health Officer, Dr. Mobsby, who proved to be one of the most hard-working men on my staff and well earned his M.B.E. With his help we collected several sanitary inspectors and vaccinators and one or two other junior Health officers. The Medical Supplies Depot came to our aid with vaccine and lymph and with a few syringes and only a dozen or so needles inoculation started, any member of the staff with a spare moment helping in the work. I shall never forget seeing Dr. Jury sitting on an upturned soap box for hours filling syringes passed to him by three members of my staff who were each dealing with a long line of refugees. How these refugees hated it, and who could blame them when needles were used until they almost had to be hammered into the poor unfortunate's arm. About forty thousand were inoculated in the first week and each man was given a typed certificate. Later we discovered that these certificates were being sold for several rupees, which in at least one instance had tragic consequences.

We sent off a boat with about a thousand labourers for the Myitkyina-Bhamo road. Every man had to show his certificate on embarkation, but by the time the boat arrived at Katha dozens had died and more were dying, all having purchased their certificates.

Although the medical staff I had collected were working splendidly, a senior European medical officer was very badly needed to control the whole work of the medical section. After repeated applications to Government, a Dr. Broatch was posted to me, an ex private practitioner from Rangoon and an old friend of mine. Within two days he was transferred back to the Army, but in that short period he was invaluable by descending on the Mandalay bazaar and looting every medical store, all of them locked and barred by the owners who had long since bolted from Mandalay. I accompanied him on some of these excursions and can almost sympathise with a burglar's choice of profession. Even though this looting occurred in broad daylight and was definitely necessary, there was quite a thrill in breaking into these locked shops and then seeing what we could find. I am almost certain Broatch enjoyed himself; I certainly did, and the result was the finest dispensary Mandalay had ever seen, including a water distilling plant.

The morning Broatch left, a very irate Dr. Jury charged into my office, exclaiming: "What sort of a doctor is that specimen we've been sent. He's impossible. I ask him for vitamin pills for women and children and he pulls down a box of anti (pronounced an-tie by the doctor) fat pills. What use, I ask you, are 'an-tie' fat pills to starving women and children." He was almost frothing with rage, so settling him on a chair in my office I visited Broatch. The Doctor's remarks are unprintable, as it appeared he had packed all his medicines when collecting them in the shops in empty cartons of Anti Fat Pills, and had not had time to sort everything out. I was very sorry to see Sandy Broatch leave, but had he stayed he and Dr. Jury would never, I fear, have forgiven each other.

A day or two after this incident, when returning from a visit to the various camps, I was met with the news that Williams had been taken to the Isolation Hospital with cholera. No relief had been sent to take Broatch's place, so after snatching a meal I drove to the hospital, a small building containing twenty beds and situated on the bank of the Irrawaddy. It was impossible to drive into the compound as the ground was covered with at least two hundred dead and dying. Inside was a shambles, all the beds were full and one could hardly walk without stepping on patients covering every inch of the floor. The only illumination was provided by two hurricane oil lamps. The only doctor, an Indian, the only nurse, a Burmese, and the Burmese ward boy were completely overcome. They had been working almost without a rest for nearly forty-eight hours and had no medicines left. The doctor was under the local Public Health Department but could get no response to his repeated requests for assistance. The Health Authorities, I discovered the next day, had disappeared. I had heard that Dr. Broatch's partner in Rangoon, Dr. Lusk, had arrived in Mandalay, so set out to look for him and tracked him down about midnight. He immediately returned with me to the hospital, where we found the staff had given up the unequal struggle and had all gone to bed. Then and there Lusk agreed to my request to join my staff and take control of all medical arrangements, accepting this hospital as an additional responsibility.

Poor Williams died the next day, but Lusk cleared up that hospital and had the cholera epidemic under control within three weeks. An Irishman, he was never weary, never depressed. I can well remember him one night, after a particularly trying day when we were all dead beat, lying back in his chair, his legs stretched out, roaring out his Irish songs with Tommy and Nancy, myself and my wife, and several others all joining in the choruses. I seem to recollect at least one visit to the dugout that night to replenish the bottle of Tio Peppe we were drinking. Lusk also was awarded the M.B.E., an inadequate reward for his magnificent efforts and for the many hundreds of lives he saved.

Another man to whom I was greatly indebted was Robert Hutchings, the Agent in Burma for the Government of India. His assistance in Rangoon was invaluable, and it was through him I obtained the whole-hearted support of the Indian leaders, one of whom remained on my staff till the end.

I remember an incident in Rangoon when it was imperative that I should get Hutchings' (the Government of India's) backing to shipping refugees with free tickets, owing to their poverty. I hunted high and low for him, eventually running him to earth in the evening at the Sailing Club, where I found he had gone out in his yacht. I chased him in the Club yacht and got his agreement as we sailed back to the Club. At Mandalay he had been a tower of strength and when leaving for a short air trip to India, left his assistant, Mr. Tyabji Junior, to keep in touch with me. An urgent request by me to Tyabji, cabled on to Hutchings, for medical supplies resulted in a plane landing within two days at Shwebo with all our requirements.

About a year later a book was published by a war correspondent, an American I think, which gave the impression that this time in Mandalay and the subsequent two or three weeks, was a complete shambles with no law and order, due to the utter demoralisation of all officials left in the country. I first heard of the author at about this time in Mandalay, when one of his despatches passed through the Censor's office with a detailed description of how our troops at the front were being sniped at by traitor Burmans hiding in the tops of palm trees. This despatch had been prepared in Maymyo, the hill station, at least a hundred miles away from the scene of the fighting, which this war correspondent had never visited. Later I heard in India he was writing his book, and, as I was staying in the same hotel, sent him a message that I should be pleased to give him any information he required. I have yet to meet this man. I bought his book, and, like most of us who knew the facts, I burnt it.

My office staff had increased considerably and we all felt very lost when a grand old man who had been my Superintendent from the start of the Department decided that the tempo was more than he could keep pace with. He was a retired Police Office Superintendent and must have been well over sixty. He went to Maymyo to collect his family, and there foolishly remained instead of making for the north. Five weeks later I was to find him sitting in a train at Naba with no hope of getting out by air, having left it too late. He and his family were too old to stand the rigours of the walk out to India, and I have many times wondered what happened to him.

Again, as so often had happened, the right person turned up at just the right moment to fill this vacancy. This time it was an Anglo-Indian lady, Marjory Murray, an expert steno-typist who had been confidential stenographer to the Rangoon Turf Club, and who had a figure which would have earned her a fortune as a mannequin. Fortunately her efficiency more than made up for the hours wasted by several of my officers who suddenly seemed to find masses to do in the office.

Another most efficient man was my Anglo-Indian accountant, an ex temporary clerk of the Accountant General's office in Rangoon. We were spending lakhs (100,000) of rupees, actually about £20,000 a week, without any of the normal red tape and sanctions from higher authority. Staff were taken on and rates of pay fixed as I considered necessary. I had so far been unsuccessful in my request to Government for sanction to a scale of pay for my staff submitted in January when in Rangoon. Fortunately,

Forbes Mitchell, the accountant, had not been in the Accountant General's office long enough to become a slave to red tape and regulations and nothing perturbed him. All day he would work at accounts preparing vouchers for tens of thousands of rupees without blinking an eyelid, and when that work was over I would find him pottering about the transport park or issuing rice or doing anything for which help was required. On one occasion getting on towards midnight, hearing the sound of a small riot from the subordinates' quarters, I went across to find two rather drunken Anglo-Indians fighting. They were too far gone to take any notice of Forbes Mitchell's gallant efforts to separate them, or even of my authority, and his joy when I sent both the combatants hurtling into a very prickly bush was well worth seeing.

The Reserve Bank was at Shwebo about eighty miles north on the west bank of the Irrawaddy and supplied us with our financial needs. Our Polson's coffee van made two trips a week, taking two or three of the staff as armed guards, bringing back each time about 200,000 rupees (£40,000) almost all in one rupee coins. Then all the girls in the office would get down to counting it, stacking it in the steel almirahs and safe in piles of 20 rupees. This was often a whole day's job, and would not infrequently be interrupted by air raids. On more than one occasion Flossie, one of the girls, rather than leave all this money unguarded would hide under the table instead of taking refuge in the trenches outside.

The second raid Mandalay experienced occurred on 3rd April, Good Friday. On that day I had gone to inspect camps being erected west of the river. These camps were found necessary as, though movement across the river was discouraged, many had got across and there was an influx of refugees from villages to the south on the west bank, such as Pakokku. These people had to be collected and camps were being constructed to accommodate fifty thousand. The largest, incidentally, was in charge of the one and only European Undertaker in Rangoon, who, on joining my staff, had handed over for our use two motor hearses in which he and his men had escaped from Rangoon.

On my return that evening down the Shwebo-Mandalay road, I passed car after carload of people making for the north. Later we could see the reflection of flames on the sky over Mandalay almost hidden by a dense pall of smoke, and on entering the city we found the main railway station a shambles and the road leading from it a mass of twisted electric tramway wires covering bomb craters and torn up tram lines. Most of this damage had been caused by a fire at the station which had spread to a truck load of R.A.F. bombs. The explosion which rocked every house for almost a mile radius had put paid to the railway station as far as any future traffic was concerned.

The Civil Hospital and bazaar had also been completely burnt out. The evacuation of the former whilst it was blazing had been carried out by my staff during my absence.

The reactions to this raid affected us very seriously. Firstly the other bazaars closed down and the purchase of food supplies became increasingly difficult, particularly fresh vegetables.

Fires resulting from the raid had destroyed large blocks of mostly wooden, or partly wooden, houses occupied by the Anglo-Indian and Anglo-Burman community. This communy in their hundreds immediately besieged my office. Most of the mothers seemed to have dozens of children and my office was like Bedlam. The children were decidedly nimble-fingered, and they treated the garden as a latrine. Many had dogs with them and if we were to escape being driven mad they all had to be housed somewhere safe without delay. Many of them had had very narrow escapes during the raid and were in a seriously nervous condition. A month or more earlier, the Civil Authorities had started the construction of a special camp for the Anglo community, but the work had never been completed and the buildings had been taken

Bombed Mandalay, April 1942

Mandalay business quarter

over by my staff and extended to form a camp for cholera patients. By midday my staff had found a delightful shady site in a mango grove on the bank of the Myitnge river, about five miles east of the town, and by nightfall all these people had been moved to this camp. Other staff collected bamboos and thatch to form temporary shelters and latrines, whilst others looted the town for bedding, crockery, cutlery and camp furniture. The supplies staff also got busy providing rather better fare than had been customary up till then for the Indian refugees,

The conditions were by no means ideal, but the weather was dry and hot, and it was a perfect camp site, was away from all bombing targets, could not be seen from the air, and the river was ideal for the children. Staff were appointed to live in and control the camp, and we hoped that the crisis had been dealt with. The next morning, however, the Commandant arrived to report innumerable complaints, two of which were that one old lady had protested most strongly at being given tea and not her usual coffee first thing in the morning, whilst another complained bitterly at the absence of bedroom utensils. Thank heaven we still had a sense of humour, particularly the staff who spent the morning in the town looting chamber pots.

This story of loot and chamber pots recalls the experience of a European who, when the final collapse occurred in the following month, had to escape the Japanese by walking from Bhamo to China. On that walk he frequently met large detachments of the Chinese Army also getting out of Burma. The only loot he ever saw them carrying was one with a number three iron used as a walking stick, a second with an incredibly dirty homburg hat, and a third with a much dented tin chamber pot on his head in place of a steel helmet.

The success of this second raid on Mandalay appeared to encourage the lawless element intent on dacoity and looting who, to divert attention from such activities, set fire every night to different parts of the town. These fires were often terrifying in their intensity as they were accompanied by a fierce wind, and the flames would roar from block to block of these very inflammable buildings. Repeatedly the transport was out to the early hours rescuing the inhabitants of these burning buildings and rushing them away to the camps. On two occasions the flames were so close that the transport park, the office and our house were evacuated, but again our luck held. I usually went out in my jeep to see what could be done, and on more than one occasion Tommy, still in his evening black trousers and white collar and black tie, would jump in beside me ready to put his hand to anything. On one night we got caught on the wrong side of the fire and had a hair-raising drive through what at first appeared to be a wall of flame.

One of our worries was an inadequate supply of Burmese 'dahs', the Burmese knife used by all labour. The Army were short of these implements and insisted on all labour provided for them being equipped with this very essential tool. Soon after we arrived in Mandalay, the American business man on my staff, Walter Voehringher, who after Rangoon fell found himself at a loose end, suggested he should go back to Prome where one of his pre-war customers had, he knew, very large stocks of dahs. I gave him money and carte blanche to get everything he could. He returned about Good Friday, having achieved almost the impossible. At Prome he found the Army in control, but in typical American fashion made an agreement with the Brigadier in charge that if he was granted permission to search for these dahs he would hand over half to the Army. The store was found in a house which had its windows bricked up. Walter got in through the roof, borrowed Army transport to get the dahs away, and then sold half of them to the Brigadier, actually getting a cheque immediately in payment. He then borrowed or stole some river craft and got to Magwe. En route he discovered one of the Oil Companies was destroying their machinery and stores, so again borrowing or stealing the Magwe Commissioner's houseboat he loaded it up with the most amazing collection of Engineer's stores, including hundreds of sheets of very precious corrugated iron. He sold his own car en route for a very nice figure, picked up a far better car, put that on the barge, and made for Mandalay. The Royal Engineers took over all the engineering stores and I was able to supply an urgent request by the Army for dahs for troops in the line and still have adequate stocks for the labour. Walter, being an American business man, then tried to sell his new car to the Evacuation Department! He was an amusing type, magnificent physique, always cheerful, full of energy and ready to put his hand to anything. I think the only thing that ever upset him when serving with me was the sight of my new Superintendent's figure, again typically American.

Whilst Walter was away I took two trips to the south. The first was the result of a report that several hundred Indian cultivators with their carts and bullocks from the Kyauktaga Grant – An Indian settlement – were moving up the main road and were then near Pyinmana. It was suggested that they might be most usefully employed in making a new road from Pyinmana on the Mandalay line through the forest to Taungdwingyi, thus linking up with the Prome-Mandalay road. I was asked to supply staff to control this labour. By the time I got to Pyinmana these Indians had completely disappeared; it was some days before we discovered that they had found a cart track running westwards and had moved across to the Irrawaddy. Had I been able to contact them at Pyinmana nothing could have been done, as the Japanese were then attacking Toungoo, about ninety miles south, and we should never have had time to complete the road.

My second trip was to Yenangyaung and Magwe to ascertain the possibility of using the An Pass, due west of Magwe, as an evacuation route. The Magwe Civil Authorities were not very optimistic as conditions on this route were very similar to those on the Taungup Pass, steep slopes with miles devoid of water and no villages en route. The Burma Oil Company, however, were most helpful and offered to lay a pipe line up to the top of the Pass and pump up water, but before arrangements could be concluded the Japanese were threatening the Pass, their advance was so rapid.

I got to Magwe just after the Royal Air Force had abandoned the airfield, the last permanent airfield in Burma. The Royal Air Force had left for India even though the Civil Authorities were still working in the District, the Deputy Commissioner's wife carrying on for some time after in the Civil Hospital. I visited that abandoned airfield and saw in the huts meals unfinished, letters partly written, and every sign of a hurried departure. Who was responsible I do not know, but it was a mistake which the Royal Air Force took a long time to live down. They, with the American Volunteer Group, had been magnificent in Rangoon, their planes were old and out of date yet the Japanese after the 25th December never dared visit Rangoon by day. It was a great pity that at Magwe they spoilt that very fine record.

At Yenangyaung on the return journey I found the Burma Oil Company taking steps to evacuate, which included the destruction of their stock of Survey of India maps. Whilst at Mandalay I had several times visited the Survey headquarters in Maymyo to obtain maps, and knew how short their stocks were. With some sheets they had only one or two copies left. I was able to save most of the Burma Oil Company's maps and took them back to Maymyo where they were particularly welcome, as by then it was realised that all the Rangoon depot stocks sent to Mandalay by railway had been captured by the Japanese.

For this trip I had used my own car, a lovely twenty-five horse power Vauxhall which had belonged to the late Sawbwah of Hsipaw. He had died in about 1938 and this Vauxhall with two other cars had been jacked up pending the settlement of his estate. During my leave in 1940 in the Shan States I had stayed with the Civil Administrator of the State – the heir was a minor – and was just in time to pick this car up for a very reasonable figure. During the Good Friday raid it was used as an ambulance and was badly damaged.

Writing of Hsipaw reminds me of a story told me by the Administrator. The late Sawbwah had been educated in England and entertained in European style. Mosquitoes, the malarial kind, were plentiful around Hsipaw, and at the Sawbwah's dinner parties little Shan girls used to squat under the dinner table and, hidden by the table cloth, fan the guests' legs and keep the insects away. During dessert it was a favourite trick for the guests to throw chocolates under the table, when there would follow a terrific scuffling as the little girls would scramble for the prize.

The Sawbwah's official palace was an exact replica, only smaller, of the King's Palace at Mandalay. His residence was built in modern style.

On my return to Mandalay from Yenangyaung, I found the Irrawaddy Flotilla Company's steamers were continuing to ply regularly to Katha, every boat being packed to capacity. At Katha there was a branch line to Naba which connected with the main railway line from Mandalay to Myitkyina. Hearing that there was considerable congestion at Katha and deciding that this town should be my next headquarters should Lower Burma and Mandalay be captured by the Japanese, I sent Major Pughe, one of my staff, to construct and control a large camp on the island just opposite the town. He was also to construct a camp at Naba and lay in large stocks of rice.

Major Pughe was another ex Indian Cavalry Burma Military Police Officer who on retirement had become stipendiary steward of the Rangoon Turf Club. He and his wife were very old friends of Tommy and Nancy and were living with us at Mandalay. Pughe had been Assistant Commandant of my Race Course camp in Rangoon. He had a gammy leg due to an old war wound and later, when the situation looked grim, I begged him to fly to India, to where shortly before he had sent his wife, as I knew he could never do the trek out. He, however, was another of the old school, and I shall always remember his reply –"No, Vorley, so long as there are hundreds of women and children waiting for planes I could never take a seat; I should be ashamed to look a woman in the face ever after." There are several men walking about in England today who should have that shame. I have included this conversation as a later chapter will give the sequel. At Katha Pughe did an excellent job and had over ten thousand refugees in his camp and another three thousand at Naba. Without the stocks of rice he had stored, thousands of us, myself included, would never have made India.

Some of my staff went with Pughe to examine, and attempt to distribute rice supplies on any of the possible routes to India in that area. At that time none of us knew exactly where these routes were. Unfortunately the collapse occurred shortly after the receipt of their report and there was no time to carry out their recommendations.

This history would be incomplete without a word about Spence. He was an Australian cockney engineer of the Rangoon Turf Club, a man with a heart of gold and also a very lurid vocabulary. He was placed in charge of the first large camp in Mandalay, where he had two or three thousand refugees. Part of the camp was segregated for cholera and smallpox patients. He stayed in that camp night and day and,

Major Pughe and Miss Flossie Theophilus

I think, felt a very personal responsibility for every occupant. I shall never forget paying him a visit shortly after we had received by plane from India a consignment of medicine called 'Pro Mistura Diarrhoea'. I found him kneeling on the ground with a little Indian child in his arms giving the kid a dose of this medicine. He looked up and said, "Ullo, sir, Gaw Blimey this new medicine is a bloody marvel. You pours it down their throats when they are 'arf dead and in two secs they sits up and says 'ullo to yer." On another day he arrived in my office with his arms full of toys which he had looted from the toy shops in the town. He was going to hold sports for all the kiddies in his camp and these were the prizes. To appreciate that story one needs to have seen the camp. Construction had not been completed and the refugees were distributed over a wide area squatting under lean-to shelters. In the centre of the camp was a small hill fenced round and kept for the cholera and smallpox patients, hundreds of them. There were deaths every day, several, and the whole camp was liberally sprinkled with lime in an attempt to keep down the billions of flies. Spence was assisted by a young Anglo-Indian lady doctor who was a very gallant little soul.

And so the show went on, up at dawn, seldom in bed before midnight, and then often having to get up to deal with the refugees from the surrounding burning areas, and always a thousand or more new arrivals in the camps daily. Living conditions were grim, as the hot weather had arrived, and with the constant fires the temperature was usually around 110 degrees. There was no water supply except from a conduit in the garden, and that was fed from the moat in which daily two or three bodies could be seen floating. Steel Brothers got their tube well working and we could occasionally get jars of drinking water, but there were so many of us that our main supply was from the conduit and that had to be boiled and filtered, and seldom had time to get cool. The electric supply only functioned for a few hours in the evening, when we could revel in the use of the ceiling fans. We had managed to loot some paraffin-operated Electroluxes, but all were required for the storage of the cholera vaccine. The atmosphere was always hot and smokey with a faint aroma of putrefaction and the flies were, as in the camps, in billions.

Yet we all managed to keep fit; we were too busy to think of ailments. I went down in agony one morning with what appeared to be cholera, but Jim Lusk mixed me an enormous castor oil and brandy cocktail which, with a tablespoonful of bi-carbonate of soda every hour for the rest of the day, made my inside a complete vacuum. It had been a nasty touch of ptomaine poisoning, but I was able to be on the job next morning.

Almost daily visitors would arrive from Maymyo en route to India. There were usually eight or more for lunch and very often the same number for dinner, and often extra beds would be required for 'stayers'. On one occasion a Forest Officer popped into the office on his way to the Tamu road and asked me to look after his dog and I at first refused his request until he remarked that he would have to destroy the animal. We kept it and eventually brought it out to India. He, Jerry, was one of the most lovable animals we have ever had, and it was a very sad day when he died in Delhi over a year later as a result of tick fever. That dog was almost human. In Delhi, where my wife shared an office with me, as soon as it was five o'clock a hooter used to go, and Jerry would go to the waste paper basket, pick up a piece of paper, and take it to my wife. If she took no notice he would lay it at my feet, and one could almost see him saying; "Come on, master, it is time to go home and then have a walk." He loved the office lift, and one day spent half the morning sitting in it going up and down.

The women and girls on my staff were superb. In addition to her job in the store, my wife ran the house, assisted by Nancy and Mrs. Pughe. Mrs. Jury with her husband was out all day and every day at the camps, their particular job being the care of the women and children. Little Flossie Theophilus, an Anglo-Indian ex school teacher, about four foot nothing high but with a will of iron and the courage of a tiger, tackled any job and anyone giving trouble. She was respected and I think loved by everyone. Years later when she was on my staff in the Civil Affairs Service, Burma, I shall never forget seeing her at a dance given in our Mess when she was partnered by the chief Civil Affairs Officer, then a Major General and later Sir Hubert Rance, Governor of Burma. He was well over six feet tall and Flossie's nose came up to about his waist. She was awarded a certificate of honour by Sir Reginald Dorman-Smith for her work in 1941-42 – she had been recommended for the M.B.E. – but I think she valued that dance almost as much as that award. There were other grand girls, tiny Lucy Canavan, a slip of a thing who looked as if a puff of wind might blow her over, yet she worked wonders in Rangoon evacuating the Homes for the Aged and the Incurables, often on the jetties all day long, and finally she walked out to India and found a husband en route. When I last saw her she was the mother of two bouncing babies.

On the 13th March I was called to Maymyo for a conference with His Excellency fixed for the following day. My wife drove up with me; we had got engaged at Maymyo in 1925 and had since spent many months in this very delightful hill station. Each October there was a Buddhist festival usually lasting about ten days. These were always Government holidays when everyone who could afford it, and lots who could not, tried to get to Maymyo for the 'October week' festivities. There were always polo and golf tournaments, usually a Horse Show, always a Government House dance and garden party, and each Government Department took it in turns once every three years to throw a dance. This was often the highlight of the festivities, as each Department tried to put up the best show, the Forest Department taking particular pride in this event.

The last Forest dance we attended had been in 1930 when almost every Forest Officer contributed towards a total of over 4,000 rupees and when we all went dressed as Robin Hood, the wives wearing Maid Marion costumes. One stalwart shaved his head and came as Friar Tuck. The Club and marquees outside had been decorated to resemble jungle scenes. Life-sized papier maché tigers peered out of foliage on the stage, similar elephant heads with eyes lit up surrounded the ballroom sambhur stags and deer grazed in low bamboo clumps at the entrance to the dance floor, whilst an enormous bamboo clump rising from a round rustic seat covered with tiger and leopard skins in the centre of the lounge hid the whole of the ceiling. Peering out of the bamboo fronds were snakes and monkeys. There was a magnificent supper helped down by liberal draughts of champagne from Jeroboams. Those were the days. Those dances must have been responsible for hundreds of marriages, mine included.

Maymyo presented a very different picture on 13th March 1942, as it had already been bombed once. Many houses were empty, gardens usually a blaze of colour were now unkempt, and normally trim hedges overgrown.

The next day I attended the conference at which was present His Excellency and the Chief Secretary, General Hutton representing General Alexander who had that morning left for Yenangyaung, Major-General Goddard, and one or two other Army officers of high rank. After being told the general situation I was asked if I would agree to accept the appointment of Commissioner of Evacuation, Burma, and be responsible for the evacuation of the entire non-indigenous population throughout the country. It seemed to me, knowing what was happening in Lower Burma and how rapidly the Japanese were advancing, that it was too late for such an appointment and that the job would be impracticable, and I aired these views. However, I was assured that:

1. Upper Burma would be held.
2. The Tamu-Imphal road would be completed by the 1st May when Army vehicles bringing in military supplies would be placed for the evacuation of refugees.
3. Air evacuation from Myitkyina had been organised to start immediately, planes being available to take out one thousand two hundred daily.
4. I should be granted two hundred and fifty seats per day on the only train leaving Mandalay for Myitkyina.

The Army, however, still insisted that there should be no evacuation via the Tamu-Imphal route till the 1st May and that all refugees except those for air evacuation must be held in camps around Mandalay.

On these assurances I accepted the appointment and that afternoon returned to Mandalay.

CHAPTER VI

Maymyo is at an elevation of about 3,800 feet, the road dropping down to the Mandalay plains in two series of twenty-three hair pin bends over a distance of sixteen miles. At one of these bends, known as 'View Point', we had a magnificent view of Mandalay and the surrounding country; on a fine day Mount Popa is the only high ground visible until away in the distance one can see the green of the Chin Hills bordering on Assam. That evening the continual fires had covered Mandalay with a smokey fog which merged into the heat haze from the miles and miles of surrounding dried up paddy fields. The sunset seen through this haze reminded one of Turner's landscapes and, though we did not know it then, it was the last time we should stand on this point and watch this very beautiful scene.

The most satisfying results of the agreement with the Army were that we were no longer working completely in the dark and that, as Commissioner, I had definite and almost unlimited authority to do whatever I considered necessary. It also removed one of my most constant worries, in that all the aged, infirm, and very young children, who could never stand the acute discomfort of a long lorry journey or, worse still, the most arduous of treks on foot to India, could now be sent off to Myitkyina for evacuation by air.

To arrange for the reception of these old people and children I sent Ricketts and Booth Russell to Myitkyina. Ricketts was a fairly senior Forest Officer with a reputation for reliability, all of which I hoped would carry some weight with the senior Administrative officials in the town, who might object to their authority being subordinated to the orders of a non-Indian Civil Service official who had been suddenly promoted to almost the highest post in that very conservative Service. Booth Russell was a rubber planter from Mergui, who had already shown that nothing daunted him. There had been a railway accident near Mandalay which had held up all trains for several days, so these two men went by jeep via Maymyo, Mogok and Bhamo, a long and arduous trip. Unfortunately my fears proved to be correct, and the senior officials at Myitkyina refused to allow these two officers to take over their allotted task.

Other staff were set to work selecting those to be evacuated by air and either entraining them at the rate of two hundred and fifty a day or embarking them on river steamers for Katha, from where they could proceed by rail to Myitkyina.

As in all retreats, nerves occasionally crack and the worst in man comes to the surface. I had seen this happen once in Rangoon and came up against two other cases in Mandalay at this time. Though constantly in touch with the European population to the very end, these were the only cases I encountered in which fear had taken complete control. One of these incidents occurred on the railway station when these passengers were being entrained. Mandalay main station had been so badly shattered that all passenger trains started from the next station down the line. It was not always easy to ensure that exactly two hundred and fifty, no more and no less, arrived at the station. They were brought to the train in lorries from the various camps and even the aged could be very nimble in hopping on to a lorry after the final count had been made. On one day three more than the sanctioned number arrived at the station and my staff, rather than disappoint the old people, gave them extra seats. Just before the train left an Army officer, newly commissioned from Government employ, arrived on the station and finding no empty compartment, completely lost all self-control and pulled by their skirts all the female occupants out of one carriage, which he then proceeded to occupy alone. I arrived just as the train was steaming out of the station to find my staff livid with rage and demanding that they should be issued with revolvers, the officer having threatened to shoot them if they interfered.

The Havildar in charge of the native guard at the barbed wire barrier over the Ava bridge also had an unpleasant experience, when a civilian touring car arrived at the barrier and five officers at the point of their revolvers ordered him to open the barrier. I was not very sympathetic when he related this story as I had reliable evidence that he had the morning before let through the barrier one thousand five hundred refugees on payment of eight annas a head.

I have included these and one or two other unsavoury incidents in this book as no one with any knowledge of human nature would believe that with their whole normal world crumbling around them and with no known escape route, everyone would behave like story book heroes. I am certain that many of my staff, like myself, were at times very far from being cool and complacent and confident of the future, but we, fortunately, were too busy or too tired to think of what might happen. In an earlier chapter I have referred to a book covering this period written by an American, from the contents of which one might imagine that almost everyone, refugees, officials and non-officials, were all alike in becoming nerve shattered wrecks only intent on getting away to safety. Nothing could be farther from the truth. The events in Burma were a tragedy during 1941-42, but that small and very gallant Army, always outnumbered and with little or no air support or re-inforcements, and the comparatively few European officials and non-officials, usually ignorant of the real progress of the Japanese invasion and with no guarantee of ever reaching India, created an epic of courage and self-sacrifice and unswerving loyalty which can compare with any page of history in the annals of our Empire.

In about the first week of April units of the Chinese Army were quartered in and around Mandalay. I first met them arriving at a village near one of the main refugee camps and was to start with most impressed with their efficiency. I had stopped my jeep at the entrance to the village, thinking this particular unit was marching through. They were spread out in a long straggling line extending as far as one could see. There appeared to be no march discipline and no order; next to, or intermingled with, a party carrying rifles and machine guns were others carrying cooking pots, bags of food or odd pieces of loot. Some of them were mere boys. Then a whistle blew and was repeated down the straggling column with unbelievable results. It seemed as if, after only a few minutes, anti-aircraft machine gun posts had been erected, fires were alight and food was being cooked, whilst along the whole length of this main street troops were sweeping the ground clean with others cleaning out the houses which had already been evacuated by the villagers. There was no fuss, no shouting or orders; everyone seemed to know his job and get on with it. I drove on very impressed, only to be disillusioned during the next few miles, as I encountered scores of the halt, the lame and the blind. They were hobbling along on sticks, some had bloody bandages which had obviously not been changed for days, others appeared so weak they could hardly walk and were repeatedly resting. No one was looking after them and no one seemed to care whether they died by the road-side or joined their unit.

A few days later, as I was driving through one of the original refugee camps which had been abandoned and destroyed, I met another Chinese unit about to bivouac. I found an officer who could understand English and explained to him that the ground was probably infected with cholera and advised him to move elsewhere. He was completely unperturbed and took not the slightest notice of my advice. In the Chinese Army life is cheap, very cheap.

One other story to prove the truth of this. One evening Dr. Lusk returned from the dispensary and remarked that we should have a corpse on our hands the next morning, a Chinese soldier in the last stages of malaria and anaemia having come to him for treatment. Lusk had bedded him down on the verandah outside the dispensary. Sure enough, next morning the man was dead. We sent a message to the Commanding Officer of the unit, which was billeted in the Civil Police lines next to our office. A reply came back that they were not interested and that we could bury the man. No enquiries were made as to the deceased's name or number, no requests for his kit or clothing. He was just another body to that Commanding Officer, easily replaceable.

That is a very sad and rather frightening aspect of what appeared to be the Chinese attitude towards their soldiers. Life seems to mean nothing to them. If thousands die there are tens of thousands more. There is no need to inform relatives, no need to maintain an efficient record office, no need to waste troops in non-combatant units such as medical or service corps. They are all merely bodies to carry arms, to fight and die, and no one could care less what happens to them.

For a short while in Mandalay the work of my department carried on almost according to a routine. Refugees continued to arrive daily in their thousands, were placed in camps, inoculated, vaccinated and fed.

During this period the labour staff were very fully employed. Demands by the Army for labour to be sent all over the country were becoming increasingly frequent. Some staff had to accompany thousands of labourers to the Shwebo-Shwegyin road, then expected to be the end of the new road from Imphal but later to be the start of our Army's retreat to India. Boat loads of labourers were sent up north whilst scores of parties were operating in and around Mandalay. Those leaving for up country all required advances of pay, whilst those working locally required payment for their labour each night. Even on the last day before Mandalay was evacuated Andrewartha and Forrest were able to provide the Fort with over four hundred coolies. These two rubber planters had for years been dealing with labour; they could talk Hindustani or Urdu and the Indians trusted them.

We had formed separate camps for the local labour supply, but with these and other camps we frequently had considerable trouble with the surrounding Burmese villagers, particularly when the lawless element in Mandalay became more violent and unchecked. These Burmese, mounted on ponies, would ride round the camps at night frequently taking pot shots with their guns at anyone they could see. If any camp occupant strayed outside he was almost certain to be wounded or killed by these Burmese dacoits, particularly by those unmounted and armed with dahs.

Daily hundreds, sometimes thousands, of refugees were sent by boat to Katha. This entailed transporting them from camps several miles from the river to the steamer jetties and again checking up on inoculation certificates. Almost all these river boats were in the charge of Indian serangs (Captains) who were always ready to make a dishonest penny. Embarkation had to be supervised and staff had to watch until the boat left the shore. Even then, more than once the serang steamed out of sight and then went inshore to load several hundreds more, at a price, and of course without any check on inoculation certificates. These serangs were all Indians, they had heard how Indian refugees had been attacked and often murdered by the Burmese, and they knew that their only safety rested in getting to India, yet they stayed working their boats to the very end.

In addition to the refugees in camps, the supply section had now taken on several other commitments. The School Hall became a shop for the issue of anything we had which was required by the remaining residents in the town. Mrs Lindop, the wife of the Deputy Commissioner at Magwe, had arrived and offered her services, and she with my wife and one or two of the girls were responsible for this issue. Realising that the fall of Mandalay was almost a certainty, we had been sending by boat to Katha and to Kyaukmyaung cases of tinned stores in excess of our immediate requirements, particularly tinned milk, of which fortunately we had a very large supply.

We were also supplying the Roman Catholic Leper Asylum with their food requirements. There were two leper asylums in Mandalay, and when the Wesleyan one closed down their patients were taken over by the Roman Catholics. These Roman Catholic nuns and the Bishop who sought sanctuary in the Asylum during the Japanese occupation had a very bad time in the latter part of 1944 and early in 1945 when the Japanese knew their days were numbered. The Bishop every day for almost a fortnight before Mandalay was retaken was put through six to eight hours of third degree questioning by the Japanese military police, and almost daily these police would arrive and insist on every cupboard being turned out, including the small bedside cupboards of the patients. When the relief officer on my staff of the military administration in 1945 visited the Bishop a day or two after the town had been retaken, that grand old priest insisted on producing his last bottle of wine to celebrate the event. This bottle he had kept hidden away down in the cellars.

Dacoity and general lawlessness were still very active, and almost nightly my transport was out. On one occasion we received an S.O.S. from the Civil Hospital, which after the Good Friday raid had moved to the American Baptist Mission School. By the time we arrived all the patients had been removed but all the furniture was required for the new quarters. The houses on two sides of the school were blazing, the roar of the flames fanned by a strong wind and the clouds of smoke making our task none too easy. There was no time to waste and we went through room after room clearing out everything. In one or two beds the patients were dead and the bodies were tipped on the floor and the beds removed. I carried out a tour round the outside of the school fence to see how much time we had before the school buildings caught fire, and found that the fire had not extended to the blocks of wooden residential houses on the west side. As I was walking near this block, a sheet of flame suddenly appeared at the ground floor windows of a house in the centre of the block. It could not possibly have been caused by a spark, and a few seconds later two figures emerged from the side of the burning building. As they ran away I fired at them with my revolver, but missed. In a few minutes the whole of this block was a blazing furnace and, with no fire fighting appliances and little water we could do nothing. By some miracle the school escaped, and the next day we were able to return, collect the dead patients and clean up the place. My staff who had been living in the teacher's quarters had spent the night on the floor of our house.

The Japanese air force were now raiding Mandalay fairly frequently. The air raid warning organisation had long ceased to function. It had never been very efficient, the sirens more often than not sounding after the bombs had dropped. On at least two occasions the 'All clear' went before the Japanese had appeared. Later, our first knowledge of a raid was a whistle sounded by the Chinese look-out in the

Police lines. Once that whistle went it was more than time to take cover, as the sentry had no hesitation in firing at anyone he saw above ground.

The Chinese enforced a very strict curfew after dark, when anyone on the roads was shot without any questions being asked. We later obtained from their Commanding Officer several large passes in the form of a red star with Chinese lettering on white cloth, which at night we wore round our arm. Before receiving these we had had to turn out one night to an enormous fire and obtained from the Commanding Officer a Chinese officer and his orderly to accompany us in my jeep. We could not talk a word of each other's language, but on my return I invited them by signs to come in and have a drink. They indicated that gin was their poison, so, passing them the bottle, we with our dwindling stocks were horrified to watch each of them fill a tumbler to the brim. The orderly stood at attention behind the officer and, with almost military precision one arm straight down by his side, sunk the lot in one gulp. The officer did the same, expressing what we presumed to be the Chinese equivalent of 'Cheerio'.

An exactly similar incident occurred shortly after, when one morning I returned from the office to find a party digging a machine gun post at the corner of our garden. After these two episodes, combined with the medical attention they received at our dispensary, our relations with the Chinese were distinctly cordial.

From dawn to dusk there would always be a seething mob round the Headquarters office. Dozens, sometimes hundreds, of refugees just arrived and waiting to be transported to the camps, petty contractors bringing foodstuffs, civilians and Army officers in Mandalay coming to buy supplies, local villagers wounded in the raids coming to the dispensary for treatment, Anglo-Indians and occasionally Europeans begging for priority recommendations from me for air passages, not that such recommendations would be of the slightest use to them when they got to Myitkyina, and Europeans and others on their way to India by air hoping to sell their cars to us. We were always short of transport and purchased a number of such vehicles. One transaction of this nature had very unexpected results. The officer concerned was an elderly invalid and had to be flown out, but required payment for his car by cheque on an account in India. The money I had collected in Rangoon from the sale of deck passage tickets had been placed to my credit in a special account in a bank other than the Reserve bank, which would not accept a 'paying in' account under my official title. That other bank had left Burma, so I gave the officer a typed official letter to the bank manager in Calcutta detailing my credits and the cheques issued. Months later when I got to India and attempted to settle Evacuation finances this letter was the only record the bank possessed of my account. On the strength of this statement the bank paid my credits to the Government of Burma.

At about this time all the officials of the Rangoon banks decided it was time to leave the country, and chartered a plane which they boarded at Shwebo with what records they had rescued. I have never quite understood why they all remained in Mandalay, as some of them had no branches in the town. I was able to purchase an excellent Diesel lorry from one of them, also stocks of Diesel oil, and after they left my wife and I visited their houses to see if there was any 'loot' which might be of use to us. We found a collection of the most beautiful silver, some of it obviously old Georgian heirlooms. Deciding that it was better in our care than to be left for Burmese looters, we removed all of it, my wife eventually taking most of it up to Katha. There it had to be abandoned and is no doubt now in some Burmese villager's house unrecognisable in its coating of grime.

News from the front was daily becoming more alarming, and though it was hard to believe that

Mandalay, like Rangoon, would fall, it was certain to be subject to continual bombing and possibly artillery bombardment, so I decided it was time for the female staff to leave. They went on 20th April by car to Kyaukmyaung from where they would get a river boat to Katha, thus escaping the possible danger of being bombed during embarkation at Mandalay. They took with them all the few valuable possessions we had salved from Rangoon. I placed my wife in charge, with instructions to pick up at Thabyetkyin, after leaving Kyaukmyaung, the Bishop Strachan's orphanage which had been evacuated from Rangoon first to Kyauktaga and then to Mogok. They had been advised to come down to Thabyetkyin on the required date, and space was left on the boat detailed to pick up my staff at Kyaukmyaung. Unfortunately, without my knowledge, the Burmese Principal Medical Officer of the Civil Hospital decided on that day to evacuate the hospital, and, without any warning or preliminary survey, took everybody to the foreshore and just as this boat was leaving commandeered the vacant space. By the time the boat arrived at Kyaukmyaung there was hardly room to move on either side of the two decks. It picked up my staff, but that story will be told in a later chapter written by my wife.

That action on the part of the Principal Medical Officer caused one of the worst tragedies of the evacuation. The orphanage missed this boat, and as the result of the delay arrived too late at Myitkyina to be evacuated by air. Acting on some almost criminally mad advice, the lady in charge decided to walk with about forty of the elder girls via the Hukong Valley to India. That route was feet deep in mud, it was thick with malaria, and there were monsoon swollen streams which it was for days almost impossible for the strongest of men to cross. Only one of that party survived. Had Ricketts and Booth Russell only been allowed to take over the care of these refugees at Myitkyina, I don't think that would ever have happened. The young orphans were taken north to Sumperabum, where they were cared for by two very brave American Baptist Mission ladies who had been on my staff in Rangoon. When the Japanese occupied Sumperabum the children were turned out of all the brick houses and sent to the village huts. Later a Japanese Christian administrative officer, put all the children back into the permanent building, held services every day, and looked after these kiddies like a father. Later they were moved up to Fort Hertz from where they were flown to India. Fort Hertz, on the extreme northern frontier of Burma, remained in British hands throughout the whole of the war.

We who were left in Mandalay after the ladies had left realised only too quickly how dependent the mere male is on the opposite sex. Sammy, my Madrassi boy, and the other servants were excellent, but our quarters seemed very dull and lifeless on returning to them in the evening. It also amazed us that there were so many absolutely essential but yet such footling jobs to be done which before one had never noticed.

Tommy had sent Nancy away some time earlier, and he had gone off to Kalaw to rescue the widow of one his oldest friends. He was far from fit, having developed a crop of very angry looking ulcers. On one of the bombing raids when the Telegraph Office had been hit, he had spent almost the whole day trying to rescue from the burning building the telegraph instruments and records. He had never spared himself in helping my staff whenever and wherever help was needed, but he was getting on in years and nature was calling a halt which he would not listen to.

I had for some time been clearing my camps east of the river and filling up the camps at Ye-U, Kyaukmyaung and Kinnu, also Katha on the west bank, though there were still several thousands to move including daily new arrivals. A large camp at Myingyan had also been closed, as it was more than ever indicated that we should have to leave Mandalay before long. With the transfer of these refugees I had also moved a large number of my staff, and in Mandalay we were reduced to the essential minimum.

By this time Mandalay was almost a dead city. The Commissioner and his staff were still in residence, so also was the Police Officer; McLean of the Agricultural Department helped by McAughtrie of the Zeyawaddy Sugar Factory had been keeping the flag flying at the Agricultural School building operating the water supply being used there by Army Medical units. There were one or two other last ditchers trying to keep things going including McLelland of the Brewery, where he was turning out beer for the Army under every imaginable difficulty, but the normal civil population had disappeared. One could go through street after street with the houses on either side burnt down to ground level or a mass of rubble from bombing. Occasionally one would see a Burman or two looking for any loot left among the debris, frequently one would come across a dead horse or cow killed in the raids, swollen, covered with flies and smelling to high heaven. It was abomination and desolation with a vengeance, and one was glad to get back to one's house and meet again living people. Most of us drank more than we should during those times, the taste of lukewarm chlorinated water was alone sufficient excuse for adding a generous tot of spirits, so was the continual bath of perspiration one lived in, due to the dry, smokey, fetid, hellish hot and burning atmosphere. Spirits had no effect on one except possibly to drive away the most ghastly fits of depression; as one drank so it came out in perspiration.

There were still one or two bright spots where normality seemed to reign. Our two messes were always fairly cheerful, so was the mess of the Irrawaddy Flotilla Company down by the foreshore, where Mr. Morton, the Agent, and his staff were working so magnificently day and night. There was always a welcome there and they would always respond to a request for another boat.

Mandalay's days were definitely numbered, and I obtained from Morton a boat to be moored in mid-stream and kept for the last ditchers from Maymyo and Mandalay in case the Ava bridge, the only road bridge to the west bank, was destroyed. He could not promise any officers or crew, but one of my officers was a river pilot and Government at Maymyo agreed to send me four European boiler inspectors for the engine room.

These four men arrived on the evening of the 25th April, and after spending the night at our mess left next morning to inspect the ship. Shortly after their departure Japanese planes appeared and plastered the foreshore where we were loading up three or four river steamers. As soon as it was possible to move Lusk and I drove as hard as we could go to the river side, but at a bridge a few hundred yards from the shore there was a body in the middle of the road. It was Davis, the Chief Boiler Inspector; hearing groans we searched around and found in the field alongside Allison, also dead, and the other two inspectors seriously wounded. Williams and Russell we got back to our office, and sent them off to Shwebo by ambulance where they both died the next day. Davis and Allison were buried close to where they were killed with another European whom we found but did not know.

The foreshore was a ghastly shambles. Two or three thousand refugees had been on the bank in the process of embarking and had stood there in a solid mass as the bombs, mostly anti-personnel, fell amongst them.

The Civil Hospital had gone; Lusk and his minions were the only medical staff left in the town. There were no spare beds, so all we could do was to clear the Evacuation Office. Files, records, Forbes Mitchell's precious accounts, all went on the floor, everyone gave up their bedding, and every vehicle was turned into an ambulance to bring the wounded back to this very makeshift hospital. My staff had been reduced to a minimum and that minimum had got used to doing almost everything, but now they had to turn into nurses, stretcher bearers, chamber maids and even sweepers. Even so there were some ghastly jobs to do; one came my way when Lusk and I found a semi-naked Indian woman literally covered from head to foot in smallpox, one forearm hanging by a thread of skin and one ankle in the same condition. Her three children, two tiny toddlers, were wailing at her side. One was used to wounds, but after carrying this pox-scarred body to the car and then from the car into the office it was days before one felt clean again.

Women nurses were urgently needed, and this lack was filled by the nuns of the Amarpura convent who had helped us so splendidly during the worst of the cholera epidemic. Though Amarpura itself was now only a burnt-out shell and had been plastered with bombs, these very gallant women had refused to move and were still from their convent daily visiting the sick in our camps. We had been helping them with food supplies. They came on this day without a moment's hesitation, only stipulating that they should be returned to the convent before dusk on account of the Chinese curfew.

The previous night we had heard that the Japanese were near Kyaukse, only about forty miles away, and I had then seen the British Brigadier in charge of the Fort to ask for news and advice. Though he was responsible for blowing up the road and rail bridges over the Myitnge river, just north of Kyaukse, he had had no news from any Military Headquarters for twenty-four hours and was as much in the dark as I was. He did, however, think it was only a matter of a day or two before we should have to get out.

So all day on the 26th, after the raid was over, we went on loading boats, trying to clear our camps and preparing for our own imminent departure which we realised might be very sudden. During the morning I heard that the contents of the Mandalay Treasury were being burnt – I believe about two million rupees. The Reserve Bank at Shwebo had long since closed down and money was getting short with us. As I got to the Treasury I found a young Indian Civil Service officer, with a Burman clerk holding a large ledger, in front of an enormous bonfire which was being fed with bundles of notes. There followed the following conversation:

Self:	"Any 100 rupee notes left?"
Indian Civil Service officer to clerk:	"What's left?"
Clerk (looking up his ledger):	"98,000 rupees, sir."
Self:	"I'll take the lot."
Officer:	"Give me your cheque."
Self:	"Here you are."
Officer:	"Thanks."
Then to his clerk:	"Chuck it on the bonfire."

And I went off with 98,000 rupees.

With the possibility of a very sudden departure, it was quite probable, a certainty if the Ava bridge was destroyed, that all of us who were left might not be able to accompany the refugees whilst I and the others would have to attempt to go up north to Pughe. Anticipating this, and knowing how communications had collapsed, I had sent two messages to my wife instructing her to take the girls to Myitkyina and make for India by air. I now sent another message by one of the officers together with 5,000 rupees for her and the other women - air passages had to be paid for - also instructions to Pughe in case I could never get to Katha. I also decided to give every officer sufficient money to enable him to assist the refugees in getting out, or, if he could not get out, to keep going in Burma. I had them all up and gave 5,000 rupees to every senior officer and three thousand to the junior ones with instructions that if they got to India any balance not expended on actual evacuation should be returned to the Government of Burma in India. How mixed was that staff has already been mentioned – rubber planters, American business men and missionaries, an undertaker, suspected remittance men, a Turf Club engineer and stipendiary steward, one who had come out of Rangoon jail, Indian merchants, and a few Government officials, yet only one out of that large number failed to refund what they had left when they arrived in India.

We did not realise until our last day in Mandalay the chaotic state of the postal organisation. On that day one of the staff suggested calling at the General Post Office in the town to see if there were any letters. There were bags and bags of them, none of the bags even opened. We tumbled the whole mass of mail on to the floor and quickly carried out a very hurried search, taking any letters for anyone we knew whom we thought we might come across; there must have been weeks of mail in that office, both incoming and outgoing.

Every boat leaving Mandalay on that day was loaded with as many cases of stores as space would allow after cramming it with refugees.

At about 6 p.m. Dr. Lusk took the nuns back to the convent, only three miles away. Two hours passed with no sign of him and it was getting dark. I sent two other officers with their Chinese passes to look for him. Shooting at night was very frequent and usually very indiscriminate both by Chinese and Burman dacoits. The bodies of two Buddhist priests shot in this manner had been lying at a cross-roads on the Amarpura road for several days. Quite a few fifth columnists had disguised themselves in the yellow robes of the Buddhist priesthood. Just as nine o'clock was striking Lusk appeared, exclaiming as soon as he saw me; "Vorley, the whole bloody army is getting out." It appeared that the road to the Ava bridge was packed with troops, transports, guns and all the usual military paraphernalia retiring to the west bank. This was the first definite indication we had that Mandalay would not be held.

Sending an officer with the news to the Brigadier at the Fort, I drove round to M.J., the Mandalay Commissioner, who though a senior officer of the Burma Commission waived all claims of seniority and placed himself at my disposal, an altruistic action which I shall always remember with gratitude. He agreed to drive immediately to Maymyo to warn everyone to get out as quickly as possible. I guaranteed to have lorries and boats available until dawn.

With the Army retreating in force over the Ava bridge it was certain to be bombed and I wanted to get my transport across as soon after dawn as possible. How long we had in Mandalay before the Japanese arrived no one knew; it so happened that a Battalion of Gurkhas carried out a magnificent rearguard action at Kyaukse and held up the whole attacking force for several days. Also, strangely enough, the Japanese never bombed the bridge; it was blown up by our own troops.

All that night without a moment's respite we were loading up boats with refugees and stores, and with wounded from the temporary hospital at our office. At the camps all remaining occupants were issued with five days' rations and either put on boats or given a chance to get across the bridge and make for the Ye-U camp; the vast majority were embarked. At about midnight the crowds from Maymyo started arriving, mostly Anglo-Indians and Anglo-Burmans, and a large number of Gurkha wives and children of the Burma Military police. They arrived at my Headquarters in lorries and cars, which were sent back up the hill for further passengers, the arrivals being transferred to my lorries, the drivers of which knew exactly which boats were being loaded and where. There was one unpleasant incident when some Indian troops rushed one of the lorries and tried to turn the women and children off. My temper was not at its best then and in dealing with that rush I kicked off the heel of the only pair of leather shoes I had left. I had not the time then to realise that apart from this pair I had only a pair of tennis shoes to carry me to India, on a march which was about two hundred and fifty miles.

Some time during that night I paid a visit to the Roman Catholic Leper asylum, hoping they would agree to take off our hands the very seriously wounded we had been looking after at our office. It was pitch dark at the Asylum situated a little outside and west of Mandalay, but in the east could be seen the glare of the flames from numerous portions of the burning town, and occasionally one could hear the faint report of rifles, a sure sign that the Chinese were maintaining their very strict curfew. Law and order had completely disappeared and it was not surprising that there was no response to my repeated knockings on the front door. I shouted and tried every door without success. In the morning we were obliged to leave these casualties in the office, but gave a letter addressed to the Mother Superior to a fourteen-year-old boy who was looking after his dying mother. In 1945 when I returned to Mandalay I heard that the nuns had given sanctuary to these unfortunate victims of the air raid.

At dawn M.J. arrived with the news that no more were to be expected from Maymyo; the last boat was sent off, the lorries returned and were then loaded with our own goods and chattels and all the stores the vehicles could hold. We took our last meal in Mandalay and collected all the servants and their wives and children, mostly Indian, and the pots, pans, kettles, baskets, and tied up bundles which all Indian servants seem to have by the dozen.

Green, the transport officer, had two days before salved from a ditch an almost brand new Army lorry and had every mechanic working on it to make it road-worthy. Other lorries went out to collect drums of petrol from abandoned Army petrol dumps, but at last, at about 7 a.m., by which time the sun was well up, we started off. Green would not be parted from his latest acquisition and, without my knowledge, remained behind for several hours, when he finally towed out of the town the unserviceable vehicle. He nearly paid dearly for his disobedience as, after crossing the bridge, he ran into a heavy raid at Ywataung from which he was very lucky to escape without a casualty.

We got across the bridge safely, every one of us anxiously glancing at the sky, but after about thirty miles I found myself nodding at the wheel and on halting discovered that several others were in the same state. As we decided to put in under the roadside trees for a short sleep, there was the sound of another heavy raid and ahead of us we could see Shwebo going up in smoke and flames. As we watched there was a sudden zooming of two Japanese planes above us, and everyone disappeared in the road side ditches or under the scrub beyond. Whether those planes had dropped all their bombs or failed to see us we will never know, but they passed on overhead without attacking us.

All of us on that drive had realised that military resistance to the enemy was practically at an end. Along both sides of the road troops, utterly worn out, almost staggering, were making their way northwards. It was no rout: they still carried their arms and equipment, and an odd one would look up and wave, occasionally shout to us, but they were grey with fatigue and lack of sleep.

After a short rest, we continued on our way to Kyaukmyaung, passing through Shwebo which had caught a real packet. Houses were burning everywhere.

The Kyaukmyaung camp seemed to be overflowing, but the Commandant had seen the collapse coming and had during the past two days moved eight thousand to Ye-U and Kinnu. There were seventeen thousand left.

We managed to find some tree cover for our transport and after a meal looked forward to a good long sleep, the first uninterrupted sleep we should have for a considerable period. Luck, however, was against us; the Chinese arrived on the west bank and their Generals came across the river and required a conference with a view to taking over the camp. Simultaneously with their arrival fifth columnists set fire to stacks of hay around the camp, stored by the British Army for their mules. Finally, having dealt with the Generals and just as I was getting down to sleep a message arrived for me to the effect that Major-General Goddard wanted me at Army Headquarters first thing in the morning. I went to sleep wondering what more trouble that message had in store for us all.

The activities of fifth columnists during this Burma campaign received considerable publicity in the English press, but most cases, I am convinced, were really attributable to enthusiastic dacoits out on their own unlawful occasions. Dacoity (robbery with violence) has for centuries been the national sport of an appreciable element of the Burmese people and, with the forces of law and order so fully engaged, this period of chaos was a Heaven-sent opportunity for these lawbreakers to give full rein to their natural instincts. The fire at Kyaukmyaung, however, was undoubtedly started by fifth columnists.

CHAPTER VII

By

HELEN VORLEY

On 4th March we moved to share a house in Mandalay which had been taken for Tommy and Nancy, and we were later joined there by Major and Mrs. Pughe. I was asked to do the housekeeping as Nancy was busy working in the Censor's office.

From the 4th March till the 3rd April life was more or less an ordered routine. I used to go over to the Evacuation Headquarters which was just across the road and help in any jobs that wanted doing. Counting out rupees was the most usual. All the labour employed in and around Mandalay were paid daily and we had to count the silver rupees into piles of twenty, wrap them in paper and then stack them in the safes and steel cupboards in the office. This monotonous work was frequently interrupted by air raid warnings, but no planes at first materialised. We all mistrusted those warnings and preferred to trust to our own ears.

On the 3rd April at about 11 a.m. I and two of the girls were cutting out tickets to be given to the labourers who were going by boat or train up country. These tickets bore the Director's rubber-stamped signature. This was stamped all over a large piece of thick paper and then each signature cut out in the shape of a ticket. I made frequent excursions to the back verandah to listen for planes; there was such a noise in the front of the office with cars and lorries coming and going, one could not hear a thing. On about my tenth visit I heard the Japanese planes, rushed down to the office with the information, when everyone made for the trenches which were some way from the building. Flossie and I thought we had not time to get there, so each hid under the writing desks, of which there were two in the Director's office.

There was the usual terrific noise and loud bangs but very fortunately no bombs fell anywhere near the office and all the men went off to help in the rescue work. I and Mrs. Pughe returned to the house to pacify the servants, who were always very alarmed whenever there was a raid. I was very worried as one dog was missing. I had taken them over to the office with me and had not noticed that Judy, the spaniel, had disappeared. I found her later that evening locked in one of the office store rooms; she had got into it before the raid, having followed me in whilst I was issuing stores. We were all feeling very worried about Tommy and Nancy as their office was in the town where the bombs had fallen and we had no idea if it had been hit or not.

Mrs. Pughe and I were sitting on the downstairs verandah having a much needed drink at about 12.30 when suddenly there was the most terrific explosion, the blast nearly blew us off our chairs. Paul Peter, our servant, who had been crossing the verandah took a flying leap over the rail, beating us to the dugout, to which we rushed, not being quite sure what might follow. We learned afterwards that a railway truck full of Royal Air Force bombs at a siding in the station had been set on fire and had blown up. A jeep with a full forty-gallon petrol drum on the back had been approaching the station at the time and, though quite a quarter of a mile away, the petrol drum had been blown off the jeep on to the road.

On that afternoon the fires raged fiercely all over the town: about 4 p.m. one large fire seemed to be coming directly towards the house, so we removed all our personal belongings and packed them at the gate as the house, being built of wood with a shingle roof like most others in Mandalay, would make a beautiful bonfire. Fortunately the wind changed when the fire was about three blocks away, and we were able to return to the house and have our tea in peace.

Whilst my husband was away at Yenangyaung the Polson's coffee van brought back from Shwebo two more lakhs of rupees all in silver coin. The safes and steel almirahs in the office were all full so the money was put in a steel uniform case and placed in my bedroom on the ground floor. The next evening I was going happily to bed, not giving a thought to all the wealth stored in my room, when Tommy and Major Pughe came bustling downstairs, their bedrooms were on the first floor, and wanted to take the money upstairs as they did not think it safe for me to sleep alone on that floor of the house with so much silver to look after. The two old gentlemen gallantly tried to lift the box, and I could not help being amused as it weighed a ton and would have taken about four hefty men even to move it. Tommy thereupon insisted that his faithful old orderly, Beer Singh, should sleep outside my door, which he did. By this time I was in such a state that I shut all the bedroom windows, and what with the stifling heat and the orderly's snores I had a miserable night.

As a matter of fact, none of us were in the least interested in money as money. We handled so much of it, also there was literally nothing you could buy with it, as all the shops had closed. It might have been pebbles we spent hours a day counting instead of thousands of rupees.

When my husband took over all the stores the Commissioner of Mandalay had requisitioned I, much to the rest of the household's amusement, had insisted on all the drink being stored in our concrete dugout. I could not bear the thought of losing it all in an air raid.

There are so many references in this book to drink that readers might possibly imagine that most of the staff lived in a state of semi-intoxication. This was far from being the case, as liquor was extremely hard to obtain and once obtained stocks could not be renewed. The few cases stored in our concrete dugout comprised the entire stock left in Mandalay, and probably in the whole of Upper Burma, and with several scores of officers both civil and military depending on us, this liquor was as precious and as constant a source of conversation as one's tea and butter ration was in England during the war. All of us, particularly the officers of the Department who day after day were working from early morning to well on into the night, were living on our nerves and reserves of strength. Without the evening stimulant we would not have been able to banish the depression and feeling of hopelessness which subconsciously was ever present, I feel certain, with all attempting to do their duty in Burma during those very trying times.

Another evening the Swedish match factory went up in flames, caught by one of the many fires started by the dacoits. Walter Voehringer, the American on our staff, was living there, and he was so busy carrying out rescue work that he lost all his own personal possessions, except one suitcase which he fortunately had kept in our house. Somewhere around midnight he arrived soaked to the skin, having walked about three miles in a raging thunderstorm. After that night he lived with us.

We had just finished a late dinner another evening when one of the girls drove up in a Friend's Ambulance jeep with the news that the American Baptist Mission School was threatened by fire, and wanted the Evacuation transport to rescue them and their belongings. My husband and Tommy rushed off in the jeep to collect the transport and I and the rest of the household got busy finding places for everyone to sleep. The last party arrived about midnight with all their remaining possessions bundled up in the sheets of their beds. All the men were black and filthy as the result of fire-fighting and everyone had a raging thirst. By then there was only lukewarm water left to dilute the more interesting liquids. Most of the men had spent hours carrying hospital furniture from the building to the lorries on the road outside and many were utterly exhausted.

Altogether, thirty slept in the house that night and the scene in the sitting room was indescribable with bundles, boxes and people on every square foot of floor space.

After the Department had taken over food supplies I was put in charge of these requisitioned stores and most of the Europeans left in Mandalay came to us for their food. Whenever anyone on the staff went to Maymyo they brought back enormous baskets of fresh vegetables and potatoes as there were no bazaars left in Mandalay. The tinned milk was rationed and only people with children or babies were allowed to have any. I soon got wise to the fact that the same babies and children appeared with an incredible number of different parents.

The Indian cook we had ran away, and I was in despair, when on the day the Banks left by air the Manager of Lloyds sent his butler to the office to be evacuated. This man had worked as Head Butler for the bank for nineteen years. He was a Telegu from Southern India, a very fine looking man and an excellent cook. He agreed to stay with us as cook.

Our chief diet was tinned soup, of which we had a large selection, vegetable curried and an occasional chicken, when one could be found. A Burma chicken was usually a scraggy bird which any man with a reasonable appetite could eat in one meal. Meal times were rather a problem as there were ten of us in the house and always several visitors, usually people who had just arrived from some place down south which had had to be evacuated. However, Sammy cooked marvelously and there was always enough to eat. He and his little wife Charlie walked out with us and insisted on taking their aged and hideous 'pi' dog called Susie with them. They shared their very meagre rations with it on the walk out and Susie was still alive when I left Rangoon in December 1946; it was then about sixteen.

Another fearful problem was the flies. I don't think I have ever seen so many thousands; the pantry was black with them and there was a distinct buzz when they were disturbed. Everything on the dining room table had to be kept covered and why we did not all die of some frightful disease heaven alone knows.

On the 19th April my husband decided that I and all the girls on the staff should leave the next day. I refused to go by boat as I knew the foreshore would be bombed sooner or later, and having already experienced the very unpleasant raid at Pyinmana I was not eager for a second one. It was arranged that Walter Voehringher and two other officers should take us to Kyaukmyaung on the Irrawaddy where we could meet the steamer from Mandalay. We were to drive by car via Shwebo to pick up two more lakhs of rupees from the Reserve Bank, the last lot we should be able to get as the bank was closing down and the Manager flying to India.

On the morning of 20th April we were up bright and early and left Mandalay at about 9 a.m. Our convoy of five vehicles comprised three cars and two lorries, one of the latter containing two steel cupboards required by the Kyaukmyaung camp for the money which we intended to collect from Shwebo. Just before we left, a Japanese 'recce' plane came over, which made us all the more anxious to be underway. The Japanese were very much creatures of habit, and their usual time for air raids was between 10 a.m. and 12 noon.

Our faithful servant, Sammy

About five miles from Mandalay there was a road junction, straight on for Rangoon and the right-hand bend for the Ava Bridge and Shwebo. At this junction, which was completely bare of trees, being surrounded by paddy fields, there was an anti-aircraft battery of five guns. Just as we reached it we were held up for twenty minutes by a long column of Chinese troops coming into Mandalay.

We were most relieved when we were able to proceed on our way, and dashed across the Ava bridge at about fifty miles an hour; all breathed sighs of relief when we reached the other shore as we felt our worst troubles were over.

We arrived at Shwebo just before lunch and had about two hours in which to eat our picnic meal in the shade of the trees beside the bank whilst the money was being counted. We arrived eventually at Kyaukmyaung at about 4.30 p.m., and were housed in a most delightful wooded Forest Department bungalow standing on high ground over the Irrawaddy. Though the bungalow was filled to capacity, we spent a very pleasant and peaceful thirty-six hours waiting for the boat from Mandalay. During the 21st we walked over to look at the new military hospital then being built. This consisted of several large huts made of bamboo and thatch, and we little realised then that events were moving so fast that this hospital would never be used or even finished.

On the morning of the 22nd, the boat from Mandalay arrived. She was one of the Mandalay-Bhamo mail boats, a smaller edition of the large Rangoon-Mandalay 'mails'. There were about eight first class cabins, four on each side, and they led out into the dining saloon. Forward of this saloon was a large covered deck used as a lounge. She was towing two flats or barges, a petrol tank flat on the port side and a cargo boat filled with petrol drums on the star-board side. All told, these barges contained ninety thousand gallons of octane spirit for the Air Force, to be delivered to Bhamo. The smell of petrol was almost overpowering.

The boat and the flats were absolutely packed with passengers. In addition to a large number of last-minute Anglo-Indian and Anglo-Burman passengers from Maymyo, the remains of the Mandalay Civil Hospital occupied the roped-in portion which had been reserved for our party. There was hardly room to move anywhere, the flats were crowded, and it was with difficulty we prevented these hundreds of deck passengers from smoking. One felt that one lighted match would blow us all sky high. Two Europeans from the Burma Oil Company, the O'Connor brothers, were fortunately on board, and they were grand in maintaining order. The Captain of the boat was an Indian serang, a grand old boy with a white goatee beard.

Mrs. Lindop and I shared one cabin and the men slept on the floor of the dining saloon. The girls of the Evacuation staff camped on the cargo flat, which fortunately had a roof. There were only two combined bathrooms and lavatories on the ship for so-called first class passengers and there was a long queue outside each one all day. Drinking water soon ran out, but fortunately I had my jungle filter with me. The Irrawaddy water was like thick black soup, so it first had to be boiled and then quite hard work was necessary to pump this boiled water through the Berkfield pump filter.

We reached Thabyetkyin on Thursday the 23rd, and found all the children of the Bishop Strachan's Home waiting on the river bank to be picked up by us. They had come down from Mogok on my husband's orders to be flown out from Myitkyina. It was one of the worst moments of my life when I had to refuse to take them on board. There literally was not space to put more than four or five additional passengers anywhere. Also the water was a problem and food was getting very scarce indeed. I was able to take on board the wife, baby, and young sister-in-law of one of the Evacuation officers, and promised to send transport back to pick up the school as soon as I reached Katha.

We were on that boat for nearly four days. Each night we tied up to the bank, occasionally loading up fire-wood for the engines. This wood was stacked on the shore at the recognised halting places. What with the smell of petrol and the heat, the nights were almost unbearable. On one day there was a terrific thunderstorm with floods of rain and all the passengers on the flats got drowned out.

I had taken on board with me cases of stores which my husband was sending from the large stocks in Mandalay for our future use when Katha became our Headquarters. Amongst these stores, which were stacked in the saloon, were some cases of gin, and all sorts of people came round and asked if they could buy bottles and I had firmly to refuse everyone. Unfortunately, the engine crew heard about this liquor, and a deputation arrived and threatened to strike if they were not given a regular issue. Thereafter there was a gin parade every morning and evening for the Indian engineer staff, and, as some bright wit remarked, the old *Chinthe*, as the ship was named, did the voyage on gin.

Food ran out, so I supplied rations, and my cook cooked for all the first and second-class passengers. Most of them had only brought rations for two days.

We arrived at Katha at about 1 p.m. on Saturday the 25th April, very relieved to have arrived safely. The journey, besides being the height of discomfort and dirt, had been most nerve-racking; we had all expected to be blown up sky high at any moment, and had been very lucky that no Japanese plane had spotted us. Just after we arrived, some lunatic rushed round the decks shouting an air raid warning and there was almost a panic.

At Katha the only transport available was bullock carts, so getting our kit and stores ashore was a very slow process.

The Police Officer very kindly asked me and Mrs. Lindop to stay with him and it was an absolute joy to live once again in a properly furnished house. His wife had departed to India but the house was still in its pre-war state and we both revelled in hot baths in water, not liquid mud. The girls were put into a very nice bungalow not very far away.

On the 29th, the children of the Bishop Strachan's Home arrived, the Katha Deputy Commissioner having gone down in his own launch to fetch them.

That evening five Englishmen turned up, having come by various byways from the Shan States. They were in a highly nervous and excited state and were most scathing at we women being still in the country. They may have known of the collapse of the 3rd Chinese Army in the Shan States, but if they did they were much too jittery to pass the news on to us.

CHAPTER VIII

On the morning of the 28th the stacks of hay at Kyaukmyaung were still smouldering, covering the camp with a pall of smoke. This must have been some pre-arranged signal as, within eighteen hours, the camp was heavily bombed.

After a very early breakfast I drove to Army Headquarters in the centre of Shwebo. General Alexander was again away and Major General Goddard, passing on the General's instructions, informed me that the Army were retiring to India, starting the next day, and that no refugees were from now on to move westwards along any of the routes to Kalewa and Tamu.

This was shattering news and appeared to me very unreasonable in view of the assurance given to me at Maymyo on the 14th April, and more so on account of the fact that a large proportion of the refugees at Ye-U and Kyaukmyaung were the families of Burma Oil Company's and Burma Railway's employees, who had agreed to carry on to the end on a promise given by the Army that their dependents would be evacuated.

I was a civilian and admit to being biased in favour of the refugee; after nearly four months of constant endeavour to get them safely out of Burma it was impossible to hold any other views. Now, eight years after, I can appreciate the reasons and concern of the military authorities which necessitated such a seemingly callous and heartless disregard of the civil population, but at that time considered I was right in opposing to the utmost such an order.

Being a civilian, I refused to obey and, so far as I can remember, the General and I discussed the matter for well over an hour, and I am glad to take this opportunity of expressing my appreciation and thanks for his patience and understanding. Fortunately we had known each other in the early days in Maymyo when I was a young Forest Officer and he was a Captain. Eventually we both compromised, he giving me till 12 midnight after which hour any refugee on the road would be turned back by the Army. He also gave me authority in writing to requisition three river steamers and two trains should such transport be required. The conversation at the end of the interview will always remain in my memory; it illustrated so aptly how in the rush of events the most important matters can be overlooked. The General had informed me that the Army were retiring via the Ye-U-Shwegyin and Tamu road. I had sent fifteen thousand labourers with some of my staff to the Shwegyin-Ye-U section and had visited the work in progress, and had also sent twenty thousand to the Tamu section, yet when the General walked up to a large wall map and remarked; "Vorley, where is this ruddy road?" I had almost as much difficulty as he had in finding it on that map.

It was the same with the routes farther north. Though for some time we had all realised that we should probably have to walk out, not one of us knew of any definite route north of Tamu, and though I had been able to obtain one or two maps of that area I had given them to Pughe and could not remember anything about them.

After leaving Goddard I had about fifteen hours in which to clear the Kyaukmyaung, Ye-U, and Kinnu camps in which, so far as one could estimate, there were about twenty-five to thirty thousand refugees, possibly more. Suspecting the worst, I had ordered that morning, before leaving Kyaukmyaung, that five days' supply of food should be issued to all the occupants and that they should be started off on the road to Ye-U, and now, on leaving Shwebo, I sent a message back to the camp to clear it with all possible speed, every vehicle being used to take the less able-bodied as far as Ye-U, where they would be well ahead of the Army when it started to move.

I drove on to Ye-U, where I found the Commandant, the Rangoon undertaker, had foreseen events and had already started to clear his camps. Passing on orders to get everyone out before midnight and to issue money to all the officers, I moved on to Kinnu, issued similar instructions, and returned to Kyaukmyaung.

Fortunately the camps were well stocked with food, sufficient for every occupant to be issued with as much as he could carry. The transport was ordered to carry on till midnight and then, on reaching the Chindwin at Okma or thereabouts, every vehicle was to be destroyed. Fortunately I had some days before sent an officer to the Chindwin to organise boats for the crossing of this river, and he did an excellent job when the thousands of refugees arrived. All surplus food at Kyaukmyaung after the camp had been emptied was to be handed over to the Chinese. All the camp and transport staff had instructions to go with these refugees and I decided to move north with Lusk and Spence.

We had had no news from the north but we knew that there were thousands at Katha, Naba, and Myitkyina, and with the breakdown of all telegraphic communications they might remain for several days in complete ignorance of the developments in the south. Goddard had told me that the change of plan was due to the complete and very sudden collapse of one of the Chinese Armies, the 3rd I think, which was holding the Shan States. I gathered that on one day this army existed as a fighting force, on the next it was a rabble scrambling as fast as it could back to China, the army commander and his generals creating athletic records in the lead. This collapse allowed the Japanese to overrun the Shan States and, by crossing the Irrawaddy they could, and did, enter Upper Burma north of, and in the rear of, the main British force.

From information my officers gave me in India some months later I gathered that by midnight of the 28th every occupant of the camps, except a few who preferred to stay behind rather than risk the journey, had been got on the road to India and was well ahead of the Army. An organisation for the care of the refugees had been formed at the India end of the Tamu route and from Tamu westwards temporary camps had been built and staff were in control. This was outside my control, eventually being placed under General Wood who also controlled the Assam end of the evacuation routes further north. Not all of those tens of thousands who went via Ye-U and Tamu had been inoculated and vaccinated; in the last rush of refugees at Mandalay and after, it had been impossible to give them this medical treatment, and consequently there was a fair number of casualties amongst them on the road. I gathered subsequently from my staff that with news of the Army's retirement to India many of the refugee camps along the route had been abandoned by their staff, the organisations presumably being in the process of closing down in the forward areas. This, of course, made it far more difficult for the refugees. Before crossing the Chindwin they had been able to augment their food supplies from stocks collected by the officer who had organised river transport, but after Okma food was very scarce. How many succumbed on the road I do not know definitely, but until the Army assumed control at Kalewa, when, as mentioned above, part of the civilian refugee organisations closed down, casualties were very few. Mr. Hutchings in his final report on this evacuation wrote: "There were according to my observation practically no casualties, and this I believe held good up to 15th May when Tamu was evacuated." From Tamu the organisation assisted the refugees with transport. It is estimated that about a hundred and twenty-five thousand were evacuated via this route; that is the estimated number of arrivals in Assam. I doubt if the casualties amongst those who reached Tamu after 15th May were equal to one per cent of that number.

Having done all that was possible at Kyaukmyaung, Lusk, Spence and I drove off on the afternoon of the 28th in two cars, again arriving at Shwebo just in time for another very heavy raid. We were fortunately on the outskirts of the town when the raid started, but en route for the station where we hoped to find a train, had to pass through the most heavily bombed area, and for the second time I had the nerve-racking experience of driving through a wall of flame. I just put my foot hard down on the accelerator and trusted to luck. One could hardly keep one's eyes open and the heat was blistering. Almost all but the Government houses in Shwebo were of wood or bamboo and street after street was a raging inferno. There had been no rain for months, everything was tinder dry.

The railway station had not escaped, but the Railway Transport Officer's staff were still at their posts. There was no train in the station or at any of the sidings and they could hold out no hope of any train arriving. So far as they knew there were no trains on the line between Mandalay and Shwebo.

Lusk and I decided to wait for a few hours, particularly as we had lost Spence, who had been in his own car. The station being an unhealthy place to stay in, we drove along the line for about half a mile to the shade of a small copse. There we found the Stationmaster, an Indian, lying on a stretcher, having been badly wounded in the raid of the 27th. His wife was with him. He could not move and it looked as if he had little hope of recovery, yet they were both cheerful though resigned to their fate. Lusk and I eventually brought them back to the station and the Railway Transport Officer's staff promised to put them on the first train north. I have often wondered what happened to them. They were so brave and seemingly content in each other's company though their whole world had collapsed and they had so little to look forward to.

Lusk and I finally decided to drive as far north as we could by car, which only meant about fifteen miles to Tantabin. There the motor road ended but we might get a train, and if that failed we could link up with some retiring Army unit. At Tantabin that evening we met a Battalion of Burma Military Police under the command of 'Tarzan' Learmond whom I had known in Maymyo in pre-war days. His Battalion was acting as rearguard on the flank of our retiring Army. He made us very welcome and we were able to give him the latest news, but I think what thrilled him most was the fact that I intended to ditch my car, a beautiful almost brand-new 1941 Chevrolet saloon. His Battalion was mounted, but with only ponies for transport his movements were very restricted. However, I wanted a haversack, so we did a schoolboy swop, my 3,000-rupee car for his 10-rupee haversack. Seven years afterwards I was introduced to a man in the bar of the Grand Hotel in Lagos, Nigeria, who remarked; "I have met you before, didn't you swop a car for a haversack at Tantabin? I was one of 'Tarzan's' officers." It is a small world.

Later we discovered a train at Tantabin station. It was a so-called Chinese Hospital train, or in other words a long line of cattle trucks packed with Chinese wounded with no nurses and no doctors; from the bandages it was only too apparent that the wounded had not been attended to for days. We discovered that they had been in that train for ten days, during which period they had no medical attention whatsoever and there were some terrible cases amongst them. Except for a small portion of his face, one man seemed to be completely covered in bandages.

In typical Chinese fashion some of the less severe casualties had got into the engine and, imagining it could run without a stop to their journey's end, had stuck their revolvers in the backs of the driver and firemen with every intention of shooting if the engine stopped. A Chinese soldier's threat is very close to action, so the driver had gone on till the engine blew up for lack of water. The engine staff had disappeared when we arrived but later poured out their woes to us. The Stationmaster, an Indian, was still at his post and was able to telegraph on my authority for an engine to be sent down from Kanbalu, which did not arrive till the next day. Meanwhile, Lusk and I found an empty truck on a siding, in which we tried to make ourselves comfortable.

Shortly after, a very harassed Spence appeared. He had been with us to Ye-U on the 27th where an attractive Anglo-Indian girl, whom he and his wife had known in Rangoon, had begged to be allowed to accompany him up north. Spence's soft heart and susceptibility to such a beautiful damsel in distress could not withstand the appeal and, having brought her back to Kyaukmyaung on the 27th, he had, without my knowledge, taken her in the car to Shwebo on the 28th - that morning. The wall of fire was too much for the girl who, we gathered, completely collapsed. I wish I could repeat Spence's description; Lusk and I were doubled up with laughter. It seemed that he had driven back to Ye-U with this nerve-racked girl's arms around his neck, his shoulders flooded with tears. He had left her there and followed on after us. The episode had been too much for him, so, leaving him in a deck chair with a bottle of whiskey, Lusk and I went to see what we could do for the wounded in the train.

I am not usually squeamish at the sight of blood and wounds, but the sights Lusk uncovered that evening were beyond all description. Many of the wounds were gangrenous, dozens of the men had not a hope of surviving, yet there was hardly a murmur or a groan as we went from truck to truck. I felt myself going very queer and had to get back to our truck, where I went down with a roaring go of fever. A couple of stiff tots out of Spence's bottle and a quinine injection when Lusk returned, put me to sleep for twelve hours, during which time I had sweated the fever out of me and by next morning I was more or less normal. Spence by that time had also recovered in spite of, or because of, the whiskey bottle being empty!

Whether the Chinese ever had a proper medical branch in their Army I could never find out. We had once before experienced the lack of it in Mandalay where a large building had been taken over as a Chinese military hospital. Part of it got a direct hit on one of the raids, when mangled dead and wounded were lying on the roadside for hours after, receiving no attention. The dead were buried by my staff, and I think the wounded were dealt with in the Civil Hospital; I did not see any Chinese medical staff there at any time.

On the 29th, after getting our truck shunted on to the hospital train, we started for Kanbalu, filling the engine with water by buckets from wayside streams and collecting fuel from any patches of forest along the line. At Kanbalu the next day we got our truck shunted on to a train which was just leaving with most of the railway staff. As soon as this was seen by the Chinese, all who could hold rifles gathered round the engine of this other train and threatened to shoot the driver and fireman if the engine moved. For a while things looked most unpleasant, and we finally had to allow the Chinese train to leave first, we following immediately behind.

On the morning of 2nd May we steamed into Naba junction; it had taken us about sixty-four hours to cover what normally took the mail train twelve hours. At Naba trains seemed to be everywhere, dozens of them, and all packed with refugees. I saw the acting Agent of the Railway, Brewitt, who in reply to my enquiry told me that my wife and the other women were still at Katha, His Excellency at Myitkyina having issued orders that no more trains should be sent further north than Naba as Myitkyina was overflowing. It was only then I heard that the air evacuation had been almost a complete failure, an average of about only two hundred instead of the promised one thousand two hundred having been flown out daily.

My camps at Katha and Naba were packed and there was hardly room in the station yard for any more trains. I also knew that at least six, possibly more, river boats, packed to capacity, were on their way to Katha; this meant at least an additional five thousand refugees must be dealt with, and thousands of them and those in the camps and trains could not possibly stand a march out to India along an unknown and unprepared route. Air evacuation had to be got going, and as Brewitt was going at once to Myitkyina with a number of cipherettes from Army Headquarters at Shwebo, travelling by a rail motor coach, I decided to go with him. I left Lusk to contact Pughe at Katha with instructions to get rice sent out along the Naba-Bamauk-Pyinbon cart track and to expedite the start of all able-bodied refugees in the camps on the trek to India.

I don't remember much of that journey to Myitkyina; I slept most of the way, but was told at the journey's end that there had been considerable excitement amongst the passengers when a wild elephant crossed the line just ahead of the carriage. I do, however, remember in my waking moments that at every station there were trains held up all packed with refugees.

That evening at Myitkyina we had a meeting with His Excellency when we did our utmost to persuade him to leave for India and make the authorities there realise the urgent need for more planes. The information on this air evacuation we had heard in Naba was correct; American planes, daily transporting petrol over the hump for the Chinese National Army, were frequently landing on the return journey but were not taking refugees as the planes were full of empty forty-gallon petrol drums. They were Dakotas capable of taking at least forty passengers. This is not a criticism of the pilots; they were carrying out their orders. One or two did in fact pick up a few refugees but something was obviously wrong in India when that sort of thing could happen with at least twenty-five thousand refugees waiting to be rescued.

His Excellency the Governor assured us that he had sent more than one senior officer to India to explain the situation and showed me a thick wad of copies of messages to the same effect which he had sent, but all to no purpose. There were several very senior Indian Civil Service officers and police officials present at this conference and finally His Excellency agreed to go himself, but at a later interview I had with him alone, he, on hearing that my wife, Mrs. Lindop and the girls were still at Katha, ordered me to return and send them up at once by the rail coach and promised to see that they were flown out, after which he would leave. This was typical of the many thoughtful acts and consideration I had previously received from His Excellency in Rangoon and Maymyo. In later months and years I heard him criticised, often severely, but during those very trying times I could not have wished for more help, understanding and consideration than I received from him. Whatever the critics may say, the Army retreated to India on the 29th April, Sir Reginald Dorman-Smith left Myitkyina on 4th May 1942, only three days before the Japanese entered the town and then only, I believe, on receipt of direct orders from the Prime Minister in England. That fact alone confounds all criticism.

The military authorities it was evident did not know in Myitkyina what had happened in the south, as up to the 4th May a new Army Headquarters was being built in the town whilst a few miles to the south in the Pidaung Game Sanctuary a six hundred-bed military hospital was under construction.

Some months later I discovered, as the result of a casual meeting with an officer who had at this time been in charge of the aerodrome at Dingyan, how successful had been His Excellency's efforts on his arrival at Delhi to speed up the air evacuation. On the 6th May that officer received telegraphic instructions containing the Viceroy's authority to requisition every plane on the aerodrome regardless of nationality. By the following morning there were sufficient planes to evacuate four thousand daily and the first plane left that morning for Myitkyina. The plane was machine-gunned and the drome bombed as it was loading up refugees, and that ended the chance of rescuing these many thousands.

Possibly at some future date the full history of the attempts to organise this air evacuation will be published. At the time we who were in Burma blamed India, some blamed the Americans; I have since been told that the Royal Air Force refused to allocate an adequate number of planes for this most vital urgent operation. Whoever was responsible should have on his conscience until he goes to his grave the death of thousands of women and children who believed implicitly that their evacuation to India was assured.

Had sufficient planes been available, Myitkyina could have been cleared of refugees in less than a week and the ghastly tragedy of the Hukong valley, to be told in a later chapter, would never have occurred.

At dinner on the 3rd, before the conference with His Excellency, I met several men I knew, one a hefty forest manager of a timber firm, aged about forty-two, who, offering me a case of whiskey, remarked to my surprise that he was booked to fly out the following morning. I accepted his offer and collected the drink the next morning, when I found him all prepared to leave for the aerodrome. I mention this incident as illustrating the inefficiency of the allocation of the very limited number of air passages and also the incredibly selfish behaviour of some of the Europeans. This particular man had for years spent most of his life in Burma on tour in the forests, he was as fit as could be, and during the previous five months had been in the north carrying out his normal duties without any of the nerve- racking physical and mental strains so many others had experienced.

Yet when I met him in India some months later he was completely brazen and not the least ashamed of saving his own skin probably at the expense of the lives of two women. There were, I am glad to record, only a few men so lacking in moral courage and sense of decency.

Tommy was one of the other type. He arrived at Myitkyina and, though well over sixty and in a very unfit state, his head and shoulders covered in ulcers, he refused to accept an air passage until he was satisfied that all those in his staff had got away. Even then, when offered a seat on a plane on the last day of the air evacuation, the 6th, he refused to accept it unless he could take with him his Indian orderly, Beer Singh, a faithful old servant, almost Tommy's age who had served with him and his family for over twenty-five years. For both these old gentlemen, and Beer Singh though a servant was an Indian gentleman in the true sense of the word, the walk to India would have meant certain death.

Before returning to Naba the next morning I met Ricketts of my staff from whom I heard of the refusal of the civil authorities to hand over to him control of the refugees. In the hope that India would respond to His Excellency's personal representations, it had been agreed at the conference on the previous night that trains should be allowed to run as far north as Samaw and Mohnyin, just south of Myitkyina, and that refugees should be kept in camps at these two places until the crush at Myitkyina had been reduced. Samaw was very suitable as it contained a large sugar factory which, with the outhouses could house many hundreds; there was excellent tube well water supply, also railway sidings. I placed Ricketts in charge of this work and he travelled back with me as far as Mohnyin. With the Japanese arriving on the

7th, these camps never materialised, but Ricketts did a magnificent job conducting refugees out along the Hopin-Somra-Manipur route to India, for which with his other splendid efforts as my Deputy over a period of five months he received a very well-earned O.B.E.

CHAPTER IX

BY

HELEN VORLEY

On the evening of 29th April I received a very hurried and undated note from my husband telling me to fly out immediately with Mrs. Lindop and the girls. I showed this note to Major Pughe, who was in charge of the Katha refugee camp, and he arranged that we were to leave by train for Myitkyina the next day. We were all very upset about this order; none of us wanted to fly as we felt we had left it too late; the aerodrome was bound to be bombed sooner or later. I kept a diary during this period and was able to take it with me to India. Reading it now as I write of these happenings, I find the following entry against the 29th: "Were told to get ready to go by special train to Myitkyina to fly out. Damn."

However, we spent all next morning trying to pack. This was very difficult as we did not know if we were allowed to take ten, twenty, or thirty pounds of luggage with us; it varied with the planes, and as there were no scales available it made things very complicated. We had just finished this unsatisfactory job when Major Pughe arrived to tell us he was very sorry we could not fly out as there were no more trains to Myitkyina. He thought we were completely mad when Mrs. Lindop and I cheered loudly. In the light of future events I think we were too, at being pleased at the thought of having to walk an unknown number of miles when we could have been in India in about two hours.

It was then decided we should be taken by car to Indaw, just down the line from Naba junction and from where the road started. It was planned to start the next day, so we spent another morning packing. We had to start afresh, as we now required stout shoes, thick socks, also shorts and shirts for walking. Mrs. Lindop and I left at about 7 p.m. on the evening of the 2nd and I was promised that the girls would follow first thing the next morning.

The bungalow at Indaw was a small Public Works Department building and was just next to the railway station. It was absolutely packed with all sorts and kinds of people, including some Army officers who had come to look at some maps which were there, and after dinner there was a discussion on the route to be taken, as it was an entirely last-minute idea.

Mrs. Lindop and I left the next morning 3rd May, being very worried as the girls had not arrived. However, the Forest Officer in charge promised to send them on as soon as possible. We went in a large American car with the gear change on the steering wheel; in those days these cars were very few in Burma and the young Forest Officer who drove us had never driven one before. There were five of us in the car and five dogs. The road was only a dry weather cart track, and as we came to the wide and shallow streams we all got out and walked across, as the bridges were very flimsy and the car liable to fall through. All went well till about 12.30, when we had a sharp, sudden and heavy thunderstorm which made the road very muddy. We had a steep hill to go up with two hairpin bends and at first we got well and truly stuck. We got out and I shut the doors to keep the dogs in and we all pushed and shoved but were unable to move the car an inch. Fortunately, a large body of military police recruits came along and they all pushed and got her out, and with their help we reached the top of the hill. Some silly ass had left one of the car doors open and all the dogs had jumped out. There was a stream running beside the road and, all being hot and thirsty, they had wallowed in it and were covered in red mud. When we arrived at our destination, Pyinbon, about 4.30 p.m. we also were well and truly mud coloured.

We drove up to a bungalow which belonged to the Forest Department and was very pleasantly situated. We were given a very welcome cup of tea by the occupants and then proceeded to have much needed baths.

The bungalow was occupied by two European Government officials who had been sent there to help and direct refugees on their way. Both of them I knew very well, one particularly so as he had been stationed in Toungoo when we were there. That evening we had a very heated argument as these two officers wanted to send Mrs. Lindop and me on with another party of refugees at crack of dawn the next morning. We both flatly refused to go, as I had promised my husband I would not go without the four girls who had been left behind at Katha. These four girls had been absolutely grand, and as they were Anglo-Indians I was afraid no one else would look after them properly.

Just before dark, Dr. and Mrs. Jury arrived with one of the girls and a Police Officer in their small car. The girl was Lucy Canavan and the Police Officer became her husband after they arrived safely in India.

After dinner we had another terrific discussion, the two officers getting very drunk and unpleasant. Finally Mrs. Lindop and I agreed to go with the party the next morning. It was against our better judgment, but we were placed in a very awkward position. These two officers, though their behaviour was so unpleasant, had been made responsible for getting the refugees on, and I knew how awkward it was when people refused to obey orders. Mrs. Lindop was terribly upset; like me, she had no idea where her husband was or if we would ever see them again, and we both went to bed decidedly sorrowful and very angry.

We had a most uncomfortable night, five women in a very small room with just the bare boards to lie on. The fifth was a hospital matron who had come with Dr. and Mrs. Jury.

We were roused at 4.30 a.m. and dressed in the dark with the aid of one small candle. I luckily had brought with me two packets of candles and we found them most useful on the walk out.

We had tea and a boiled egg each, standing round the table on the verandah, and it was whilst we were consuming these that the two officers calmly announced that they also were leaving that morning with the party but could not take Mrs. Lindop and me as we had no food supplies. At Indaw we had sorted out and packed two small boxes of essential stores but the car had been so laden that there had been no room for them and Mr. Smith, the Forest Conservator, had promised to send them on by the first car following us.

We were both aghast at this news, particularly when we realised that Dr. and Mrs. Jury, both well over sixty years of age, and Lucy Canavan were also to be left behind. With everyone streaming out in haste, we had no idea what the reaction of the Burmese villagers might be; we thought we might easily be murdered. Mrs. Lindop and I each had a revolver, and when these two creatures insisted on leaving us I almost shot them both, certainly one of them who was the ringleader. I still wish I had done so; he deserved it. When we realised that they meant to go without us, we made them leave some tea, milk, sugar and biscuits, as we had no food of any sort. They with their party left at about 6 p.m., these two 'gallant' men, who were supposed to stay on in the bungalow to help others on their way, leading. I am not normally vindictive, but must admit to feeling disappointed about two months later when I discovered these two men had arrived safely in India.

The Police Officer who had arrived the previous evening kindly agreed to return in Dr. Jury's little car with a letter for Mr. Smith. This letter was an S.O.S. asking Mr. Smith to send some men to take us out as we were stranded. During that afternoon, Angus McLean and McAughtrie arrived to escort us out. I knew them both very well as we had been in Pyinmana with Angus, and McAughtrie had been in charge of a large sugar factory at Zeyawaddy quite close to Toungoo, where we had also lived. I was so pleased to see them that I literally fell on their necks and hugged them heartily, in spite of the fact that they looked like escaped jail birds with shorn heads and stubbly bristly chins. Later, three Irrawaddy Flotilla Captains, the Police Officer and the remaining three girls also arrived bringing with them our boxes of stores, much to my relief.

Before their arrival, Mrs. Lindop, who could talk Burmese very well, had got hold of the caretaker of the bungalow and, giving him some money, had arranged for him to go to the village and buy chickens and eggs, and his wife then cooked us a very good Burmese curry for breakfast.

After the others arrived we had a consultation and decided to leave early the next morning. We sent for the village Headman, a very fine old Burman, and he promised to supply a bullock cart to take our few possessions to Mansi.

We set out about 6 a.m. on 5th May and did about seven miles of very pleasant walking along a village cart track, arriving at quite a large village where we had breakfast out of tins. Being May, it was the peak of the hot season, so we rested there till the afternoon, when we intended to carry on and try and make Mansi that evening. As we were waiting, a jeep drove up, and to my joy it contained Booth Russell, Andrewartha and Bob Forrest, all Evacuation staff whom my husband had sent to find us and conduct us on the walk out.

Booth Russell told us we were to go straight to Mansi, another seven miles, and he would use his jeep as a ferry service. It was just as well he had the jeep as otherwise one of the Flotilla Company skippers would have been a casualty the first day. He was a very large and very fat man with flat feet and obviously quite unused to walking on rough roads. After we had done about three miles, I found him lying beside the road, purple in the face. He assured me he could not walk another step. I stayed with him till the jeep returned and we hoisted him aboard and he reached the bungalow safely. Mrs. Lindop, I and two men walked the whole fourteen miles, and I was very tired and stiff when we arrived, not really having walked for more than a year.

The Mansi bungalow was a huge timber building with a shingle roof and was the jungle Headquarters of the Bombay Burma Trading Corporation. There was an enormous living room complete with a large bar, comfortable chairs and even beds. The servants were still there and were delighted to see us; they rushed out, got masses of chickens and pounds of rice, and we had the most marvellous meal, our last real meal for many a day, though we did not realise it at the time. This feast was preceded by hot baths for everyone, which helped to unstiffen us, then we gathered around the bar. There were quite large stocks of drink and we all spent a most convivial evening, finding two bottles of champagne which were duly opened and drunk with much enjoyment.

We all went early to bed and slept like logs. My husband and Booth Russell arrived about 2.30

a.m.; no one heard them though they crept into the bungalow, had a look at all the sleeping beauties, and retired for a spot of sleep under a large tree in the compound.

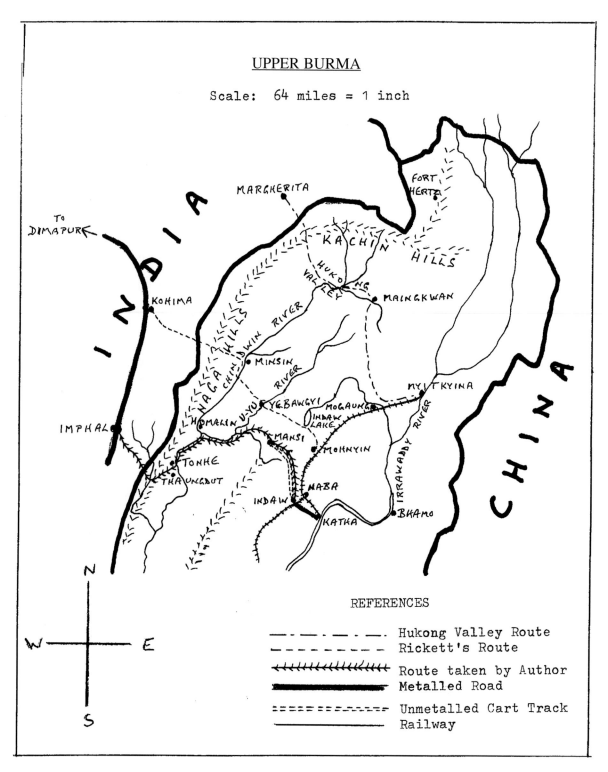

UPPER BURMA

Scale: 64 miles = 1 inch

TO DIMAPUR

INDIA

MARGHERITA

FORT HERTZ

KACHIN HILLS

KOHIMA

HUKONG VALLEY

MAINGKWAN

NAGA HILLS

CHINDWIN RIVER

MINSIN

MYITKYINA

YEBAWGYI

MOGAUNG

INDAW LAKE

IMPHAL

HOMALIN

U-YU

MANSI

MOHNYIN

IRRAWADDY RIVER

CHINA

TONHE

THAUNGDUT

NABA

INDAW

KATHA

BHAMO

N

W   E

S

REFERENCES

—·—·—·—·—	Hukong Valley Route
-------------	Rickett's Route
‹‹‹‹‹‹‹‹‹‹‹‹‹‹‹	Route taken by Author
▬▬▬▬▬▬	Metalled Road
==== ==== ====	Unmetalled Cart Track
—————	Railway

Map of Upper Burma

CHAPTER X

Brewitt and I were nearly twelve hours on the return journey from Myitkyina on 4th May. There was only a single line and 'line clear' signals were telegraphed normally from station to station. At many of the stations the staff had disappeared, between some of the stations the telegraph wires had been removed, whilst at every station there was at least one train waiting to steam northwards.

We got in to Naba at dusk to find Lusk waiting for us on the station full of the news of another stroke of luck. Wandering around Naba he had met a Chinese General who had been a lecturer in medicine when Lusk was studying at Edinburgh University. This General was in charge of the Chinese medical organisation, if such a thing existed, but he did possess four lorries which he handed over to us as he was making tracks for India. This was now our only transport as Pughe had had to depend on Burmese bullock carts.

Interrupting Lusk with this excellent news, I told him we must collect all the ladies as they were to go to Myitkyina at once, only to hear that they had all started that morning by car on the first stage of the walk to India. There was no proper motor road out of Naba but a car could use the cart track for about forty miles. Having His Excellency's promise, I decided to go after them and bring them back. The lorries were unfortunately at Katha, but after about three hours we obtained the loan from a Chinese General of his very ancient saloon in which the battery was almost on its last legs. Somewhere around 11 p.m. we set off, frequently halting to examine one of the many hundreds of groups of refugees sleeping beside the road. The road was thick with dust and at every halt a dust cloud would envelop us. After about four hours we got to a wayside bungalow which we found full of officers. They covered the floor with hardly an inch separating them. Fortunately one whom I had known in Rangoon woke up and, in answer to my question, told us that all the bridges ahead were down and that there were hairpin bends around which a car could not possibly be driven. He was wrong, but we did not know that then. We did not know if the women had halted after their drive out or if they had tackled the first march, and with our petrol getting low we regretfully were obliged to turn back.

At Naba Lusk had secured an empty wooden house of four rooms, previously the residence of a Railway subordinate, and had converted this into our office and Headquarters. There I met Booth Russell; how he had got down from Myitkyina, and with his jeep, I have never been able to make out – there was no road – but there he was full of confidence and good spirits and I gave him the job of finding those women and conducting them out to India. So far as I could see, his jeep was full of bags of silver rupees and bottles of drink, both very essential.

After a meal we returned to the station to try and get into telegraphic communication with Katha. The station was packed with refugees, trains were at every siding and others were arriving. I took a walk down the line to see if I knew any of the passengers, and found in one very crowded compartment the Hamilton family. They had been very foolish and, instead of making straight for the north after I saw them last at Prome on the 25th, they had gone to Maymyo. There was a slender chance they might get to Myitkyina in time to be flown out, and I was able to transfer them to a train just leaving for the north.

There being no response to our enquiries from Katha, we got into our car and drove there, going direct to the station. As we got on to the platform the drone of Japanese planes could be heard, and almost at once well over a dozen of them appeared round the bend of the river, flying very low. The driver of a train full of refugees standing in the station had the sense and courage to drive down the line, we ran as fast as our legs could carry us, burying our noses in a ditch on the side of the road; there were no trenches. Bomb after bomb seemed to rain all round us, but again our luck held.

We returned to the station via the Treasury. The Deputy Commissioner when the raid started had been burning all the notes and sending bags of silver out in canoes, to be sunk in the Irrawaddy. The raid had killed the Havildar and one or two others of the Military Police guard, and as we passed we saw staff throwing bags of silver down the large well in the compound, watched by some Chinese troops who had arrived in the town. The station had not been touched, so we moved off to the foreshore where several boat loads of refugees had just arrived. Here we found a repetition of the Mandalay raid. There were, I think, four boats each having disembarked about eight hundred to a thousand just as the raid started. These passengers had sought refuge under some enormous Kokko trees along the bank and had stood there whilst anti-personnel bombs cut them to pieces. The sight of one woman severed completely in half will always be with me. There was little we could do, having no medical kit with us and not even knowing our way around the town. One little incident will illustrate the native's imperviousness to pain. An Indian came up to us with a piece of bomb about five inches by three inches sticking through his hand. Lusk pulled it out and with a strip from the man's dhoti bandaged up the wound. That done, the man smiled and gaily set off to walk to India, about three hundred miles away, though we told him to try to find the hospital.

We eventually found all my staff and final arrangements were made for three of the four lorries to work all out taking the occupants from the Katha camp beyond Naba. All would get food, of which there were ample stocks at the camp, whilst the fourth lorry would collect rice from a dump of nearly a thousand bags at Naba and distribute it along the Naba-Pyinbon-Mansi route. It was arranged that all the staff should join me at Naba the next morning, 5th May, when we ourselves would start the march out together. I begged Pughe to return to Naba with me and catch a train for Myitkyina from where he could fly out, but he was adamant in his determination to attempt the trek to India. By this time my Commandant had arrived up river from Kyaukmyaung with the news that the last boat from that camp had arrived at Katha. These boats had arrived with barges on both sides and before all the passengers had been able to disembark one or two of these barges had received direct hits in the recent raid.

Pughe and his staff were confident that they could get everyone on the road by the next morning so, as there was nothing more we could do, Lusk and I started back for Naba. As we left one of the staff remarked that some boats recently arrived were full of Army boots, and I was still hobbling about on one heelless shoe. We made for the foreshore where we found that the bilge cocks in all the boats had been opened and they were gradually sinking. My need was urgent, so Lusk helped me in a feverish search in the hold of these sinking ships. The information had been correct; there were thousands of boots, crates and crates of them, but not a single pair larger than nine, and I took a large ten, so we continued our journey, watching with amusement for a while Chinese troops going down the well at the Treasury and bringing up bags of rupees.

At Naba we found Brewitt trying to clear the station of the dozens of trains, hampered at every turn by lack of staff and by the interference of the Chinese troops who were trying to go north. The Chinese General in charge, for some unknown reason, imagined that Brewitt and his officers were going to leave at any moment, so placed an armed guard with fixed bayonets to follow Brewitt wherever he went, even to the lavatory where they stood at the open door. Earlier these Chinese troops had insisted on the departure of a train which was far too long for one engine to pull. After leaving Naba, the engine, after going about half a mile, failed to take a fairly stiff gradient; the troops had then uncoupled the last few carriages, which had run backwards into the station crashing into another train and causing many casualties. Whilst I was on the station some more Chinese jumped into the cab of an engine and, with their revolvers cocked, forced the driver to move off though the signal was against them and we had not received the 'Line clear' from the next station. It got round the first bend and had a head on collision with a train from the north. Dozens of refugees in that train were killed or wounded and the railway staff had a terribly hard job trying to clear the line. With this behaviour of the Chinese troops it was becoming increasingly difficult to retain the subordinate railway staff, and large numbers of them disappeared, for which no one could blame them. Brewitt and his officers worked wonders, but that evening the situation became utterly impossible, the line was partially blocked, communication between station telegraphs had ceased as the staff had gone and there was practically no staff left at Naba to run trains, but the armed guard was still waiting to shoot Brewitt if he attempted to move away from the station.

Finally that evening a meeting was arranged with the Chinese General, when he was made to realise how hopeless conditions were. I went to that meeting but, after about three hours by which time no decision had been reached, it was quite evident to me that no more trains would, or could, run, so I returned to the house we had taken over, made final arrangements for moving out the next day and got to bed, my first sleep for about forty-four hours.

CHAPTER XI

Although so short of sleep, we woke up at dawn on the 5th May as there was still a lot to be done before we could leave Naba.

One of the first and most unpleasant jobs was to deal with the camp of Anglo-Indians and Anglo-Burmans on the outskirts of the town. There were between five to seven hundred occupants of this camp, all fairly elderly parents with large numbers of children. They were all incapable of surviving a two hundred and fifty to three hundred mile trek to India. Whilst I had been at the conference the night before, Lusk had been informed by a senior Army officer that all British troops in the area were starting their retreat to India at 9 a.m. on the 5th. There was, therefore, no hope for these Anglo refugees. I called up the leaders of the camp and explained to them the situation; it was one of the hardest and most unpleasant tasks I ever had to do; it was impossible to escape the feeling that one was letting them down. One of the leaders had been on my staff in Rangoon and had left to look after his large family. My old Superintendent and his family were also among the occupants of that camp. It is difficult to find words which can adequately express my admiration of the manner in which these leaders took the news. There were no recriminations, no unpleasant criticisms; they accepted the facts and we discussed calmly what was the best action they could take.

Fortunately there were still ample stocks of tinned food, particularly milk. All these supplies were handed over to them, also all the spare shotguns and other arms and ammunition we could lay our hands on. Shortly after this discussion, a senior Forest Officer arrived, not on my staff and offered to get one lakh (100,000) of rupees from India to be given to the head man of Mawlu, a village tract nearby, to be spent on the care of these refugees who had decided to leave the camp and disperse to the surrounding villages. I was all in favour of getting the money, but wanted it distributed amongst the leaders of the camp as I did not trust the honesty of the headman. My wish, which was supported by the leaders, was overruled. I gathered later that this Forest Officer had his way and, from some of the refugees whom I met again on our return to Burma in 1945, I learned that none of the money ever got to them. Luckily we still had a good deal more silver than we could carry and all our spare cash I handed over to the leaders.

Meanwhile every half hour or so lorries would arrive from Katha, disembark their load of refugees at the start of the road, and return for more. Lusk and I and Spence sorted out all the stores and kit we had left, limiting our respective loads to absolute essentials and selecting only the most nutritious of the tinned stores.

At Katha on the 4th I had been in the house in which I understood my wife and the girls had been billeted and had searched around for the steel trunk my wife had taken up from Mandalay. It contained possessions which I did not want to lose, including my 1914-18 medals, but it had completely disappeared.

Four years later, an Indian Civil Service officer told me the sequel to this search. He had been administrator of the District in the Civil Affairs Service in 1945, and on one of his tours had been offered a cup of tea by a Burmese Township officer living many miles out of Naba. He was rather surprised to find the table covered by what had at one time been a valuable Chinese embroidered tablecloth. Absent-mindedly fingering the edge of this cloth he came across a large embroidered 'V' and, on turning over the edge saw my name on a Cash's name tape.

We had decided to have a really good breakfast before we left and the cook had prepared sufficient for all the staff arriving from Katha. In the meantime we had tried to contact the other officials who had been at the conference, but found that most had left. The staff from Katha arrived about 9 a.m. with the news that they had done all that was possible, and we were about to sit down to our last civilised breakfast for at least a month, possibly for ever, when a Japanese plane came over flying very low. It was only a 'recce' plane, but experience had taught us that bombers were seldom very far behind such scouts, and any delay in leaving might be suicidal. I think we all managed to swallow down a bowl of hot tomato soup, and then we piled into the lorries. The commandant from Kyaukmyaung had managed to bring his car with him on a boat as far as Katha, and five of us got in this with one on each front mudguard. We intended to use these lorries so long as there was any sort of track, so took petrol and oil, also our very faithful Indian servants, and any spare space we loaded up with refugees.

I led the convoy in the touring car and halted every half hour. The road was packed with refugees which, with the ruts and dust, kept our speed down to about ten miles per hour, and even then the dust cloud completely blotted out the car in the rear. We were all together without mishap at the entrance to Bamauk and fixed our next halt at Pyinbon about ten miles ahead, but on arriving there I found that the lorries had got lost.

Writing a note to the Resident of Imphal in Assam warning him to prepare for the arrival of at least twenty thousand refugees by any possible route over the Naga Hills, I sent on the car with the other occupants with instructions to go as fast as they could and, if possible, get to India ahead of the hordes on the road and get doctors and supplies sent down to meet us. At the Pyinbon Headman's house I found several senior Government officials, and from them learned that the Army had taken control of the evacuation. They, the Army, had issued orders that all civilian refugees were to be kept in one camp at Pyinbon and the military in another, and they had also taken over all the rice supplies dumped in the Police lock-up in the town.

I decided to wait until my lorries arrived – incidentally they contained all my stores and kit – but at about 4 p.m. we received further information from the Army that they had been ordered to be across the Indian frontier by the 15th and they were off at once. An officer handed to us the keys of the Police lock-up and advised us to get going without delay.

This officer had a little Morris 8 which he was leaving at Pyinbon, so I decided to go back to Bamauk to see what was happening to my staff. Also we had the news that a Commanding Officer of a Battalion of the Burma Rifles at Bamauk had threatened to take over all the civil rice supplies placed on the road for refugees and I wanted to try to prevent that.

The journey back was a nightmare; the wretched little car had choked jets in the carburettor and stopped every few miles or so. There were no tools and I had to tinker about with only the help of a penknife. I had left at about 4 p.m. and was still three miles from Bamauk at 7 p.m. when a bridge I was crossing collapsed and the car and I, fortunately gradually, sank through the broken boards to the dried stream bed, again fortunately, only a few feet below. There were hundreds of refugees passing and they quickly got the little car on the road again; the shock must have done the carburettor good as I had no more trouble.

I found the Burma Rifles Commanding Officer; the Battalion was on the point of leaving, and I was relieved to hear that the rice requisitioning rumour was false. I then met an Indian Civil Service officer, always known as 'the Orphan', and from him heard that he had sent my lorries back to Naba for another load of rice. It appeared that a certain officer, who shall be nameless, and who had had instructions to lay down rice along the road, had cleared off and had joined up with the staff of General Stillwell's Headquarters, who were also making for India along this route. I found some of my staff and left instructions for them to bring the lorries through to Pyinbon, where I would wait for them. Picking up my faithful Madrassi, Sammy, and his wife, Charlie, I returned to Pyinbon taking about two hours as the carburettor started giving trouble again.

I made for the Headman's house where I had left the senior officials who had promised to await my return, only to find that they had cleared off without leaving any message and, even more annoying, taking the few tins of stores they had given me; my food was still with the lorries. It was then about 11 p.m. (5th May), and I had had nothing since my bowl of tomato soup. There was no moon and one could hardly see a yard but after losing my way several times I got to the rest house, a wooden building on posts with the floor about eight feet above ground, and found there the Mandalay agent of the Imperial Tobacco Company, a lady missionary and several other Europeans sitting down to a hearty meal, but completely ignorant of the route they should take to their destination. Accepting their most welcome invitation to join in the meal, I later got from the Headman a bullock cart and sent them off on the next stage to Mansi. There was still no sign of the lorries, so I decided to await them on the side of the road.

Once again luck was with me as, coming across a jeep, I fell over the owner who was sleeping on the ground beside it, and to my relief heard the infuriated voice of Booth Russell demanding what the hell I thought I was doing. Replying in very much the same words, I discovered that he had spent the whole day ferrying my wife and her party from Pyinbon to Mansi and had now returned to see if he could contact us.

On my suggestion that we should drive at once to Mansi and tell my wife to wait for us all, his action was to stretch his arm up to the back of the jeep, bring down a fat-looking bottle, and remark: "You need a spot of this." I did, even though it was Grand Marnier, in fact we both needed several spots. Eventually, we decided to leave Sammy with a message for my staff, which message we also left with the Headman, and push on to Mansi. Booth Russell told me the women were making for Kyauksegyi on the U-Yu river one march beyond Mansi, and I arranged that all the staff should meet there.

We got to Mansi about 2 a.m. (6th May) and went direct to the Bombay Burma Trading Corporation's forest bungalow, a very large roomy teak building. It was in darkness, but, creeping in, we found all the women fast asleep on the floor. They were dead to the world, so we crept out and got down to sleep under a large tree in the garden.

That morning I discovered that McLean and McAughtrie were with my wife, also Dr. and Mrs. Jury. They had all had a very trying time which has been related in the preceding chapter. Whilst we were having tea before setting off there was the sound of heavy traffic passing the bungalow, and on looking out we saw a number of Army vehicles driving past. Two of them were Chinese, the rest British; later that day we met them all abandoned where the cart track ended and became merely a footpath.

We pushed on to Kyauksegyi but soon realised it was further than we thought. We were walking along the bank of the U-Yu river and spent the night on an island near the far bank and so away from the stream of refugees including large numbers of Chinese troops. We slept on the ground under the stars, the first of quite a number of similar nights that followed. During that day the jeep went back and forth helping the older members. The road gradually got worse until it was only a footpath, and a very rutty and uneven one at that. That first night was the first chance my wife and I had had to share our experiences since she left Mandalay. Having had no news of me, my arrival that morning had been most unexpected. Booth Russell had been a real God-send, and without him I don't know what would have happened. The next morning we went to a good site on the north bank where we decided to wait until all the rest arrived.

Whilst camping on the sandbank on the previous night, I had got in touch with some elephant attendants of the Bombay Burma Trading Corporation in their camp near the riverside and discovered that a herd of the firm's elephants were grazing a few miles away. I did my utmost to persuade these men to collect their animals and to accompany us, as this transport would carry all our food supplies and also the older members of the party, particularly Pughe. Unfortunately, these elephants were grazing some distance away and as their attendants were not all present the animals could not be collected; it was a very great disappointment.

Shortly after waking on that morning of the 6th May we heard the martial tramping of feet and watched General Stilwell, his staff, and about one hundred Indian labourers carrying the kit, striding down the path on the opposite bank getting out of Burma.

That afternoon the staff arrived, having to abandon the lorries shortly after Mansi. Booth Russell had tried to drive his jeep down the stream until it went into a hole and he found himself sitting in the driving seat with water up to his knees.

There were about fifty of us, which included the tobacco Agent, the missionary, two Irrawaddy Flotilla Company's skippers, and several others not on my staff, including one incredible old boy, at least sixty, who had originally started as a refugee from Hong Kong, from where he had travelled by boat, on foot and by car to arrive at Singapore. He escaped from there to make Rangoon, where he had obtained employment with the Irrawaddy Flotilla Company, and had now walked from Katha. On account of a very blistered heel, he was wearing a shoe on one foot and a boot on the other, the odd shoe and boot being hung round his neck on a piece of string. His only food supply for the entire journey was one packet of Quaker Oats.

We held a meeting and went into the question of food supplies, only to discover that almost all our stocks which had been parked at Bamauk when the lorries returned to Naba had been stolen. We had a fair amount of rice, a very few dried lentils, some tea, sugar - very little - one tin of Klim, not full, one tin of Glucose 'D', and a small tin of Quaker Oats, which when opened proved to be rancid. My wife and I reduced our clothing to two pairs of shorts, two shirts (one on, one off), two pairs of stockings and a towel each. We also had one Aertex blanket each and one green canvas sheet about seven feet by six feet. We had a comb apiece and I kept my shaving gear. My wife had her jewelry and some money in waterproof silk round her waist. She also kept one pair of slacks and, what proved most useful of all, a Burmese loongyi, which is like the Malay sarong. We had an Army pack each and an Army oiled-silk cape which we had looted from an Army depot at Katha, and I also carried an old 9mm Luger automatic pistol which I had picked up at Passchendale in 1917. My wife had a small .32 automatic.

Everyone else cut their kit down to a minimum, and we then divided amongst us the coin which Booth Russell had salved from his jeep. Silver rupees are heavy, so we each took thirty, and some of us also had a stock of a hundred rupee notes; I still had five thousand intact. The rest of the coin we threw into the river.

It required little imagination to realise that the chances of some of the older members of the party walking the whole distance were very remote. None of us knew what we were in for, but I had a fair idea that we should have to do about a hundred miles along this river and the Chindwin and then possibly the same distance over the Naga Hills, and these hills were an unknown quantity. I knew they would be steep, very thickly wooded, probably malarious and possibly uninhabited, but worst of all I knew that the rains were due to start very shortly and constant rain in those hills meant malaria, pneumonia and death for many of us unless we could reserve our strength and unless we could find habitation.

The U-Yu river was deep enough for bamboo rafts and if the old people could raft down to the Chindwin river their strength might last out for the hilly march to Assam. We therefore divided the party into two, roughly about twenty-five each. Lucy Canavan who was supposed to have a weak heart and certainly did not look strong enough to tackle the whole journey, was included in the elderly party. Dr. Lusk was put in charge of that party and I took care of those who would do the whole journey on foot. We decided to spend the next morning helping to make rafts, but on waking found that Lucy had disappeared. Her future husband – they were not then engaged – was with us and had been included in my party. He had protested and wanted to stay with Lucy but none of us thought the affair was serious; he was known to have a roving eye and Lucy was a very attractive little thing. However, it was serious, and rather than be separated these two had gone off on their own; it was a risky but very brave effort and they deserve all the happiness they were very definitely finding when I met them again in Delhi, now married.

The rations were divided up amongst us and my party left on the afternoon of the 8th. Men and women were about equal in number. We had been fortunate in persuading some Indian refugees to come with us and carry some of the kit. They agreed to throw away most of their personal possessions on payment of Rs.100 at the end of the walk; we also promised them daily wages of Rs.1/- plus a bonus.

As our party of twenty-five with five dogs left the camp at Kyauksegyi I had another amazing stroke of luck. We had to cross the river to the path on the far side, and on reaching the water's edge we found masses of kit abandoned by Europeans who had obviously used this camp before our arrival. Amongst that pile of clothes I found a pair of almost brand new Dunlop rubber golf shoes, size 10½. They fitted me perfectly and I was able to throw away my old heelless leather shoes which were then in the last stages of collapse. Those Dunlop shoes are with me now; without them I should never have been able to complete the two hundred odd miles we had ahead of us. My wife had also found a large bundle of new Burmese silk loongyis or skirts which had no doubt proved to be too heavy for the refugee to carry. The ladies all took one as they are an excellent substitute for a bathing dress when they had their daily bath in whatever stream was available for our morning halt. The only trouble was that the dye was not fast and as my wife's garment was a mixture of vivid pink and green checks she emerged a brilliant shade of pink for the first few days after her bathe.

One lady was most anxious to get on quickly and join her husband who was known to be ahead of us. He had been one of the officials I had met at Pyinbon on the 5th, and she and I had some rather bitter arguments. My plan was to be up at dawn, have a small meal and walk till about 11 a.m. when the heat made walking very trying, then to rest till about 3 p.m. and after a cup of tea walk till dusk when we should have our evening meal. I also insisted on a halt every hour and reckoned we should cover about fifteen miles a day, quite sufficient with the Naga Hills ahead of us. She wanted to go on all day which I firmly refused.

The first few days were very trying as soon after the start the path petered out and we had to take to the stream, walking from sandbank to sandbank often paddling up to, and over, our knees in water for half a mile or more. Nothing can be more tiring than constantly pushing against water except possibly wading through the thick loose sand on the sandbank. My wife and I still had our dogs, they had gone with her to Katha. Jerry, the magnificent black cocker, Judy a black mongrel, three-quarters spaniel and a quarter terrier, and Vicky a wire-haired terrier. This last was born on the day the five British destroyers attacked Narvik, and each pup was named after one of the destroyers. 'Vicky' was short for 'Vixen'. This little terrier was full of pluck but started the march with a slight attack of distemper. For these dogs the wading through water for us meant swimming for them, probably covering six or more miles each day in this manner.

And so we went on sometimes sleeping on a sandbank at night, sometimes on the banks of the river. We preferred the sandbanks as one could dig a hole for one's hip and make a comparatively soft bed for oneself. Usually my wife and I spread the tarpaulin under us to keep out the damp but when there were occasional showers we had to get up and fix it above us on sticks; if there were no sticks we just crept under it. Water we got from the stream dosing it liberally in our water bottles with bleaching powder which will kill all infection. The taste is foul, particularly so when one is rather inclined to be on the safe side and put in too much.

On the second or third day Bob Forrest, one of my labour officers, developed dysentery; he was constantly disappearing and daily, almost hourly, looked weaker but not once did he complain. It was about the second day of the attack that we discovered what was wrong and found that one of my Indian doctors had the necessary injections with him. However, on opening his case he found all but one ampule smashed, but that one seemed to do the trick, or at least kept the disease in check till we got to India. Andrewartha, my chief labour officer, was also another worry as he had had phlebitis a few months earlier in his leg and there were signs that the swelling was starting again. Luck was with him and it never got too bad.

Every day, usually on the short cuts cutting off the corners, we passed refugees who were dead or dying. I always remember one body; his back was to the path but we could see that he was one of the better class Anglo-Indians. He had died of cholera and though we felt we should search his body to find out who he was none of us had the courage to touch him. That sounds absurd after all the infection and filth we had been in contact with for months, but I suppose we were all keyed up. We had so far escaped, there were probably only two or three weeks more to go before getting to safety and we were not taking any more risks than we had to; but I shall always regret not having found out his name and being able to notify his family when I reached India.

Luckily Lusk had brought with him a supply of quinine and had given me half, and every night I issued five grains to each member of the party. We did not have a single case of malaria on the actual march though several suffered from it afterwards, one or two fatally.

On the 11th as we were having our morning tea a thunderstorm started, the first heavy rain for months and a sure sign that the rains were very close. It continued for some time but we carried on, arriving about midday at Maingkhang; by then we had covered about forty-five miles. There we found the missing husband and one or two other Government officers. They had been busy making rafts and rather to our disgust they cleared off with the lonely wife whom we had looked after, taking the labourers with them and leaving us two partially completed rafts. We were all rather abnormal in those days. Quite apart from all we had been through which must have affected our nerves and mental stability, we were all tired out before starting the march. This particular husband had done magnificent work in his District, only leaving when the Japanese were almost on his heels, and he must have been as tired mentally and physically and as tautly strung as we were.

We worked on those rafts that afternoon (11th May) and started off on them at about 4 p.m. Two days before, along one of the short cuts, we had met a Chinese trader with a long string of mules and ponies. He was one of the regular traders who, year in, year out, travel down from the Shan States across the Naga Hills to Assam and back, selling, I suspect, mainly opium. He did not appear to realise, or care, that he was walking straight towards the Japanese, and we had considerable difficulty in persuading him to sell one of his ponies which he did eventually at a most exorbitant price. On this animal we loaded our rice, and on the afternoon of the 11th getting this beast on to one of the rafts was a most amusing episode. We succeeded eventually, and as we slowly but surely floated with the current down the river, smiles appeared and everyone felt that half our troubles were over. Now and again the raft stuck on sandbanks but that only meant a pleasant cool dip in the river pushing them off again; and there were roars of laughter when, in trying to jump on the raft, my wife went head over heels backwards into the river.

When we passed through the jungle we found it full of monkeys, the large grey kind with black faces. We seldom saw any but heard their whooping all round us and noticed the branches swaying as they leapt from tree to tree. These were the only wild animals we encountered except a snake which bit one of the carriers the following day. The man did not die but had a very swollen leg for a day or two. On one sandbank where we halted for the night we found tracks of leopard, tiger and wild pig, and there was one track of a solitary bison. They were all three or four days old; the stream of refugees must have frightened all the wild game away for miles.

That night and the next we slept on sandbanks after our usual supper of tea followed by rice boiled in water. A more revolting food than rice boiled in water without any milk or salt is hard to imagine. One evening we tried mixing it with dried lentils and boiling the two together, but that was even more nauseating as the lentils came out as hard as bullets. We only had one saucepan, a huge affair; a second one had been stolen. We started off with making the tea in it; that meant mixing the tea, Klim and a little sugar all together and boiling it up. Then when everyone's mugs were full the saucepan was cleaned out and the rice boiled. At this time we were having about one cigarette tin of rice per person per day; our dogs getting a little from everyone, did quite well.

By the 13th we imagined we must be nearing the Chindwin river and the stream was quite a sight as there was a procession of rafts of all shapes and sizes. One very small raft was occupied only by an elderly Anglo-Indian lady and her daughter; they waved to us but seemed quite content to be left on their own.

We had all done marvellous calculations of the rate of the current multiplied by the number of hours' travelling and achieved most satisfying results, so when that afternoon we stopped at a village we were a very sorrowful crowd on learning that as the crow flies we had only covered about twenty miles. This wretched river had twisted and turned all over the countryside and we could have accomplished more had we walked instead of rafted. It had however been a pleasant change and rest and that night we enjoyed a rather better meal, getting a few extras at the village, and slept in the dak bungalow. On one of the bends that morning we decided to send the pony across by land as it was getting very fidgety and was smashing up the raft. We sent one of the most reliable Indians we had with the animal and that was the last we saw of it. The chance of a free ride to India on the back of a pony was too great a temptation for any Indian labourer.

There had been another rather amusing experience about two mornings before, when one of the girls noticed that one Indian coolie always took the smallest of loads, and seemed to find considerable difficulty in getting on to his head a small suit case of his own from which he would not be parted. She called me over to watch the performance and I ordered the man to open the case to find it full to the brim with silver rupees. There were hundreds and it was almost too heavy for me to lift. That was the last day he worked for us.

On the evening of the 13th whilst at this village of Nyaungpuaung we heard shouts of joy from the camp of Indians who were with us and discovered that my sweeper, an excellent man, had found his wife and child. He had lost her at Mandalay and now found her walking through the village with a crowd of refugees.

That afternoon we took a path cutting off an enormous bend in the river and in the evening got to the outskirts of Homalin. During this march we had to cross a deep swiftly flowing stream, the only bridge being a fallen tree about three feet in girth. There was no handrail, the river was roaring down only a few feet below and unless one was used to such acrobatic feats it was rather alarming. My wife had an extremely bad head and balance for such bridges and on our years of jungle tours I had got used to her making miles of detours or walking waist deep through water in preference to attempting such crossings. This river was well over six feet deep and there was no alternative route so I stayed behind to help her across.

As I expected, it completely defeated her, but when she realised that the only alternative to crossing was to be left behind she made the attempt and with me in front of her and Bob Forrest behind, walked over without a murmur. It was a gallant effort as I knew she was terrified. I had had to be brutal and threaten to leave her behind.

On the way down from Myitkyina on the 4th, I had seen on the station at Mohnyin one of Steel Brothers' timber managers who knew upper Burma, particularly the Chindwin area. He had told me that after Homalin there was a fairly good path to the Indian frontier which he thought was properly aligned and had been kept clear, and he was fairly certain that it connected with a well-graded path on the Indian side. This is what I had been making for and gathered we should have to go through Homalin and cross the Chindwin a little above the town.

Imagine our disgust on finding a large notice at the entrance of the town signed on behalf of General Stillwell forbidding any civilian refugee to enter the town or proceed along the path to India. We were not in the mood to worry very much about notices but we presumed that this was the route the retreating Chinese Army would use, and we had had several contacts with this Army during the past few days. Any village the Chinese passed through might have been a village of the dead. Every villager had vanished, every fruit tree had been stripped bare, every garden had been denuded, there was not a fowl or a duck left but there were always mounds of feathers. We had seen one such visitation, with the troops as they slouched through the village firing at anything and everything on two or four legs except the villagers themselves, though regardless of whether any villager was in the line of fire.

To be fair about them we did meet one splendid unit. They passed us as we were resting at the midday halt. The officers were with them and at the rear were half a dozen or so carrying on bamboos the wireless unit complete with generator. They had their midday halt a few hundred yards beyond us, and after they had passed one lady discovered that her shoes, which had been drying in the sun, had disappeared. She walked along to one of the officers and complained and the shoes were restored in a few moments. His control over those troops was magnificent. We then got friendly with him and he turned on the wireless, when we heard to our dismay that the Japanese had taken Kalewa and were moving up the Chindwin. That had been on, I think, the 11th so we knew that we had little time to lose.

On the 14th we were in a very awkward position, either to disregard the notice and risk the Chinese, or respect the notice and move down the river toward the Japanese in the hope of making Tonhe before they arrived; as we had discovered there was another path to India from that village. That we chose the second alternative will indicate our feelings about the Chinese Army. Some miserable man had stolen my topee whilst I was asleep so I bought a large Chin hat from a villager. These hats are about two and a half feet wide and are made of bamboo and palm leaves. As my wife's topee had become like pulp with all its wettings she also obtained one and when later it rained for days on end they were almost as good as umbrellas.

We therefore re-crossed the U-Yu river and went down the path on the east bank of the Chindwin, sleeping that night in Myintha village. The next morning after a short walk, we found some canoes and, after searching for the owners, eventually did a deal for them to paddle us down to Tonhe where we arrived just after dark that evening, the 15th. Our first contact was one of the Government Marine steamers and barges on which we again met 'Tarzan' Learmond who had brought his mounted Military Police across from Tantabin by a different route.

We went into the village which was crowded with refugees, every house was packed, but after about half an hour's search we discovered an empty zayat. A zayat is a wooden hut, usually open sided, put up for travellers and usually erected by some wealthy Buddhist to earn spiritual credit. It was rather surprising that this one building was empty, but we all trooped up the wooden steps and made ourselves comfortable on the bare floorboards. Some of us searched around for wood for a fire and then we discovered a corpse under the floor and not too new a corpse either, but worse still he had died of cholera. That was enough; we all cleared out and went back to the village to see what we could find.

By luck we met the Agent of the Chin Sawbwah of the State and he invited us to his house, a large wooden building in which all the living rooms were on the ground floor, the upstairs being used as a store. He seemed to have all his friends and relations staying with him, but gave us the upstairs which was rather like walking into a scene out of 'Chu Chin Chow'. There were enormous jars filled with every imaginable spice and grain. Sacks and sacks of rice and lentils and most welcome of all to us masses of jaggery, native sugar boiled from sugar cane. He provided us with tea and a meal of rice and other native dishes and let us help ourselves to the jaggery. This is the most nourishing and strengthening food one can find. I believe that in the first Chindit show with General Wingate when his troops had to find their way in scattered bands to India, many only survived by obtaining from the Burmese villagers supplies of this jaggery.

The Agent was most helpful in giving us information on the route ahead, about which we knew nothing.

We decided not to dally but move on first thing the next morning so, feeling for the first time for several days really replete, we got down to sleep amongst the mice, the spiders and all sorts of creepy crawly things in this store, and slept well.

CHAPTER XII

We were not particularly cheerful as we started off from Tonhe on the morning of the 16th. From the information given us on the previous night we had about a hundred miles to do; that in itself was not very alarming but we had also been told that there were some fierce hills ahead of us and that water would be scarce. We also remembered the cholera victim under the hut the night before; that meant the epidemic was ahead of us on the track and water would be infected.

On emerging into the village street at our usual early hour my wife was greeted by various Englishmen who all addressed her by name; she failed to recognise any of them as they all looked utterly different with scrubby chins. She thought it extremely clever of them to recognise her, imagining she must have looked equally scruffy.

Deciding we would try to get to a village each night I led the way as I could talk Burmese and might be able to get a hut lent to us. Bob Forrest acted as rearguard to assist stragglers. He appeared to have recovered from his dysentery and though a slow walker he was sure and steady. Also by halting every hour I could get everyone together and thus not find at the end of the day that we had mislaid one of the party.

From Tonhe the path was fairly well defined and ascended a comparatively gradual slope, but after about a mile became overgrown and indistinct and in places was only a mere goat track. Even allowing for the constant rain on subsequent days and the steep slopes, that first march from Tonhe was, I think, the worst. It appeared to consist of a succession of ridges, one after the other, each one higher and steeper than the one before and each one seeming as if it was the last. We soon met and passed other refugees, all Indians or Anglos, most of them foolishly carrying as much as they could hang round themselves or load on their heads, and many with small children hanging to their mother's skirts or trailing along behind. It required little imagination to realise that many would never see Imphal.

We plodded along until about 11.30 a.m. when at the hourly halt my wife lay down on the ground and said she could go no further. We all tried to cheer her up, and realising that it was now downhill and that a stream should not be very far ahead, she managed after about ten minutes to get up and continue the march.

After about a mile we reached a stream which, like all the other streams we had passed, was dry. There were thousands of people sitting and lying everywhere, many of them in a long queue waiting to take their turn to obtain water from a tiny trickle which was oozing out of the far bank through a small bamboo pipe about half an inch in diameter. This must have tapped a small spring. After searching around I found a comparatively level spot where we were able to sit down and wait for everyone to arrive. My wife and Bob came in last, she immediately collapsing on the ground and looking absolutely done in. She murmured: "I'm finished, I can't go on," and then appeared to be semi-conscious.

This was so unlike her that I was more than worried. For years she and I had toured in every dry season and she had thought little of camp moves from nine to twelve miles every two or three days, whilst in 1931, when we had to run away from the rebels during the Burma rebellion, she had for several days walked all day through jungle, often only following game tracks. One of my assistants once remarked:

"You know, Mrs. V., you're no speed queen but you always get there." She was slow but never up till now had been defeated.

She was in fact one of the first Government Forest officers' wives to tour regularly in the jungle with her husband, which might be partly due to an incident at the beginning of our married life. After our marriage in Calcutta Cathedral we were invited to stay in Rangoon with the Chief Conservator of Forests before travelling up country to where we had been posted. At dinner one evening our host, a bachelor, turned to my wife and said. "You know, Mrs. Vorley, I always say that a Forest Officer married is a Forest Officer ruined" implying that they frequently returned from their jungle tours to comfort their wives who had not been prepared to endure the rigours of life in the jungle. My wife was never going to have that said about her husband! When our son was born in England and accompanied us to Burma at six months old, he was even packed off in the dry touring season by ship with his godmother to stay with his grandmother in Calcutta until the next rainy season.

Wondering what to give my wife to help her recover, I remembered the Glucose 'D' and mixed her a strong concoction with Klim milk powder. After this she slept and on waking I tried her with a plate of porridge which, though rancid, I thought might revive her. It was a foul looking mess but Bob and I persuaded her to swallow some of it. It was not till several days later that she told us the mixture was so disgusting that she had thrown most of it away when we were not looking.

We had to move on that afternoon as this was the last place to select for a night's halt; apart from the shortage of water, level ground was so scarce that we were cheek by jowl with the hundreds of other refugees, many of whom were almost certain to be infected with cholera. This stream had been the halting place of thousands in the days before our arrival and the surroundings stank of defecation.

Whether it was the Glucose 'D' or the nauseousness of the rancid porridge I cannot tell, but after an hour or so my wife sat up and appeared somewhat recovered. By 3 p.m. she was ready to go on; the stench alone was sufficient to make anyone who had an ounce of strength left decide to get away.

We did about another five miles that evening, rather slowly as we were all tired, and I remained behind with my wife to help her along. Though not as bad as we had experienced that morning, the path still went up and down a series of ridges until we eventually arrived at a collection of about half a dozen bamboo and thatch houses known as the village of Thanan.

Just before we arrived at this village a little incident occurred which I have ever since regretted and wish I could forget. We met the lady who had left us with her husband on the 11th, the same lady who wanted to walk all day and cover not less than twenty-five miles from dawn to dusk. They also had to abandon their rafts, after which it appeared she had had her wish and they had trekked through the heat of the day without any halt with the natural result that her husband was down with a touch of the sun. There was nothing we could do particularly as they had some other officers with them, but we were feeling rather sore over the raft incident so expressing our somewhat dubious sympathy we walked on. It was a rotten gesture but then none of us were normal at that time.

At Thanan village the inhabitants had disappeared but refugees seemed to be everywhere. Finding one hut reasonably clean I went in search of water. This tiny village was situated on the side of the hill near a stream down which the water normally flowed over a series of solid rocky ledges. With the dry weather still with us the water had long ceased to flow and there were now only a few green scummy pools under each rocky ledge. Worse still was the disgusting stench of stale excreta indicating that these

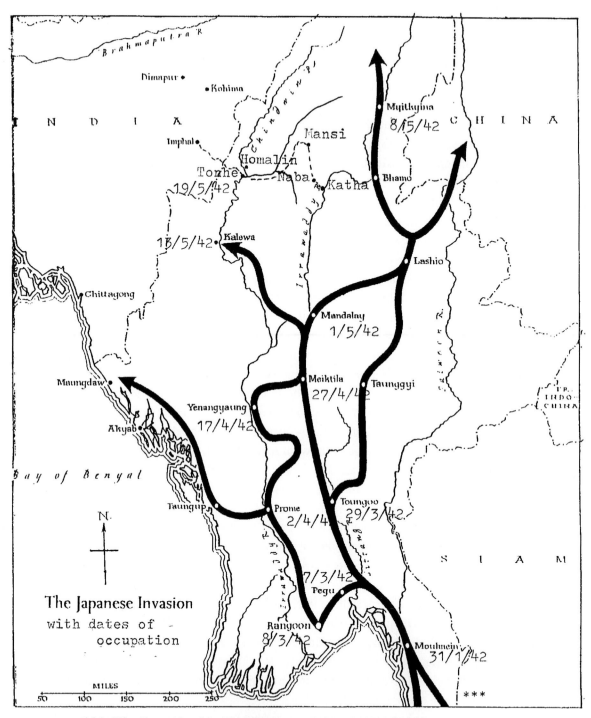

The Japanese Invasion
with dates of
occupation

*** The Japanese invaded Burma at Victoria Point 450 miles south
of Moulmein on 9/12/41.

Map of Japanese invasion of Burma, 1941/42
(author's escape route ---------)

pools had been used by thousands of refugees ahead of us. However, it was the only water supply and if well boiled would be drinkable. In its natural state it was not even fit to be used for washing.

I had a look round the other huts and found a British soldier, I think he was a private in the Gloucesters, very sick indeed with dysentery. He had been left by a party who had gone on ahead as he was too ill to walk. An Indian servant was looking after him. This was a moment which will always stay in my memory, a moment when one felt utterly helpless when there was so much one wanted to do. We had no medicines, we could not carry the poor fellow with us, he had just got to be left and one could only hope that death would take him before the Japanese arrived. The next morning we heard from a passing soldier that a rearguard under the command of a Brigadier, whom I knew, was only one day behind us, so I left a written message for the officer with the Indian servant. I doubt whether anything could have been done to save this man.

By the time I got back to the hut our evening meal was ready but even after considerable boiling the water tasted foul and none of us ate very much. The ladies, however, were quite cheerful having discovered a thick pile of straw in their hut and they were all anticipating a nice soft bed for a change, whilst the unfortunate men would be obliged to be content as usual with the hard ground outside. Shortly after our meal the ladies retired but within a few minutes came and joined us having been chewed to bits by fleas with which the straw was alive. They must have brought quite a number of these little friends with them when they left the hut as they all complained the next morning of a very restless night. My wife had made an amazing recovery and before going to sleep that night had told me how splendid Bob Forrest had been, helping her along when she was feeling so very ill.

We started off again early on the 17th and, after crossing a small stream, found ahead of us a hill completely bare except for grass and a long line of struggling refugees toiling upwards and never seeming to end. That hill was a nightmare; it must have taken us the best part of three hours to get to the top. We would walk for about fifteen to twenty minutes and then rest. We passed the Agent of the Railway whom I had last seen at Naba surrounded by his Chinese guard. He was resting with other railway officers. They passed us at our next rest and so it went on seemingly for hour after hour. There were refugees resting along the entire route on both sides, many never to get up again. Years later I met an officer who had walked down this hill during the re-occupation of Burma and he told me how the track was lined with skeletons. When many of our party were almost at their last gasp we suddenly heard the gurgling of water. Some Heaven sent Samaritan had fixed up a split bamboo conduit from a stream about a quarter of a mile away to spill out on to the side of the path. Without that water thousands would never have got to the top of that hill. We all filled our water bottles and had for the first time for days a drink of real clean spring water. It was such a joy to drink water that had no bleaching powder in it; this gives the water a foul taste and I think increases one's thirst.

During our walk down the U-Yu river we had filled our water bottles by merely dropping them in the stream on a string as we walked, and then adding from a little bottle a dose of bleaching powder the strength usually depending on the dirtiness of the water or the proximity of any dead bodies. The result occasionally tasted like pure bleaching powder and except that it was wet was the most disgusting drink.

When we eventually staggered to the summit at an altitude of nearly 3,500 feet, we were cheered by the sight of a well-graded and well-defined footpath and realised that we had now crossed over the Indian frontier. It was the one bright spot in what up till then had been a hellish day. The start that morning could not have been more inauspicious and gloomy, as added to the depression at having to leave behind the private of the Gloucesters we discovered on waking that during the night all our remaining stocks of rice had been stolen; we had nothing left but our tea and milk and these were running very low, particularly the Klim. For two or three days our tea had only the faintest colouring of milk.

It was too cold at the frontier to rest so we pushed on, entering early that afternoon a Naga village called Kanpat. This to our joy was still occupied. I routed out the Headman, a dear old boy only too pleased to see an Englishman and even more pleased to find an Englishman who could talk Burmese. He could not have been more helpful; he bustled around finding a house for us, he collected a crowd of women and started them pounding paddy to provide us with rice and when I asked if we could get any meat he told me to try and shoot one of the village pigs scuttling about everywhere. It sounded simple but I chased one of those confounded animals for about half an hour, under houses, through hedges and fences taking pot shots at it with my 9mm.Luger automatic. I very much doubt if I hit it once, or if I did I think my ammunition was so old that the bullets probably did not penetrate the skin. Anyhow the Headman took pity on me after a while and brought out his own shotgun which did the trick.

We had a marvellous feed that night, the first real meal since leaving Naba, and we cooked enough to provide us with a meat dish for the next day. The dogs also enjoyed this change as they had bones to gnaw and obviously looked as if they thought life was not so bad after all.

I was then in my nineteenth year in Burma and in all that period I don't think I had ever met a jungle villager who was not always helpful, always polite and always very pleased to see an Englishman. It is only when one gets down to the semi-civilised areas adjoining main roads or railways that one meets the insolent bad manners of the partly educated who are always the ready tool of the seldom more educated political agitator.

Before leaving Kanpat on the 18th we found stuck in a tree a note from the 'Orphan', of whom I had last heard at Bamauk, giving the details of our route ahead with advice on where to spend the night. This was most helpful.

We started off on the 18th with light hearts, it was pouring with rain, it was damned cold but our tummies were full and we had it seemed only about another fifty odd miles to go. However, at about the second hourly halt, Flossie came up and asked me to look at the foot of my superintendent – the one with the beautiful figure. Flossie had seen it the night before and was horrified, so was I when the sock had been removed. The whole of the heel was raw and must have been in that state for days. It was not just an ordinary blister, there was a festering wound about two inches wide and this girl had carried on for days in agony without a murmur. That was typical of the pluck all these girls had shown for the past five months. I could not do very much except clean up the wound and put on a dressing of sorts but the girl said she could carry on and did so.

It would be impossible to remember all the instances of courage one came across on this trek. One or two remain in one's memory; Lucy Canavan's effort in tackling the march alone with the man she loved; an old grey bearded Indian with his young wife or granddaughter, his worldly goods on a very aged and decrepit bullock and a tiny toddler, a son or grandson, perched on his shoulders. Hutchings in his report tells the story of a young Indian couple with two children on the Tamu road. The wife was tired out. The husband would walk a few hundred yards carrying their bundle of clothes and rations and taking the elder child. Then he walked back to his wife and picking up the younger child in his arms would slowly help the wife to the point where he had left the bundle. Then whilst the wife rested he went on gain with the elder boy and bundle. Again and again the process would be repeated and he had been doing it for forty miles. There were many cases of courage and devotion such as this.

Those on the route who earned our greatest respect were the Gurkha troops with their families. We passed dozens of these stalwart little men, every one of them with his complete kit, rifle, bayonet, water bottle, haversack and full pack with more often than not one of his children perched on top of the pack. Behind would follow his wife, carrying the family's worldly possessions, also probably a baby and holding a toddler by the hand. They always had a cheerful grin as one passed them; they were magnificent.

All our troops unfortunately were not so well disciplined. At Tonhe the night before we arrived a large dump of stores in the Headman's house had been looted by British troops and we had met several small parties from whom we were glad to get away. There were, however, two outstanding detachments which passed us, one was a small body of Inniskillings, bare to the waist but still carrying their rifles and still maintaining some remnants of the march discipline they had been trained in. An even better crowd was a detachment of Royal Marines. How they got up to Katha and for what reason I cannot imagine, but there they were with their officer, still carrying most of their kit and still maintaining their magnificent Marine discipline.

In our little party the Anglo-Indian girls were outstanding. They were always at my heels first to arrive, and would at once get down to making a fire, cleaning out the hut and getting a meal ready. Flossie was usually the ring leader; she never seemed to be tired, always had a cheerful word for everyone or if, as on one occasion, she caught someone trying to wangle more than his fair share of the rations her tongue would lash out and she would tear him to bits. For some days we were down to half a cigarette tin of rice per person per day.

During that morning's march I noticed that our wire-haired terrier Vicky was not with me. At one of the hourly halts I discovered that she had dropped back, for a while had followed my wife and then had collapsed. My wife had to go back along the road to look for her and found her utterly miserable and unable to go any further. Vicky had not been at all well when we left Katha and since then had frequently been wet for hours on end and of course had had only rice to eat like all of us. My wife picked her up and carried her for the rest of the morning.

From Kanpat we dropped down to the Yu river, a delightful wide and fast running stream about waist deep in the centre but with lovely deep rocky pools. We heard afterwards that when the monsoon started the river rose very considerably and that a lot of people drowned trying to get across. The Royal Air Force eventually dropped a long rope which made it possible for the refugees to get to the other side without disaster.

All of us were badly in need of a bath, our clothes even more so. Leaving the ladies near the path the men moved up stream behind some rocks and proceeded to have a washing day of ourselves and our clothes. It was boiling hot out of the shade and our clothes would dry in an hour or so.

As I was naked as the day I was born and just about to wash my shorts Charlie, my boy's wife, peered round the edge of the rock and remarked: "Master give me clothes, master no fit to do washing, Charlie do." Charlie was not her correct name, she was a Madrassi from Vizagapatam and all Madrassis have names about a mile long. We all called her Charlie, even Sammy did, and we were all very fond of her. She had stayed with us in Mandalay and she was always ready to do anything: help cook, act as lady's maid, nurse to anyone's children and now my washerwoman. There was an awkward moment when, having finished bathing, I wanted something to wear, only to find Charlie had draped all my clothes on bushes yards away from the river and all I had was a most inadequate towel.

No one, however, was worrying about sartorial effects so, clad in the minimum of clothes, feeling for a change really clean and wholesome, we enjoyed our breakfast under the shade of the trees. Luckily none of us went exploring till after our meal, as one of the men then found a corpse on the bank about 50 yards away from us, another cholera victim. Even though bathing and washing each day had not been possible almost every male member of the party, so far as I can remember, shaved every other day. The ladies must have retained their powder compacts as I cannot recollect seeing shiny noses first thing in the morning. Considering how very few clothes those ladies had with them it was amazing how spruce they kept or at least looked. The missionary lady had only a thin blouse and skirt; she had failed to bring any change of clothes with her, yet she always managed to look neat.

Before we moved on in the afternoon a British officer with the advance party of the rearguard I had had news of, arrived at the river side. He told us of an ambush by Chinese or Burmese dacoits on the Wuntho Pinlebu route when several officers had been killed.

We set off again at about 2.30 p.m. and my wife managed to find an Indian refugee to carry the terrier. Walking up one of the hills we passed a poor old Indian woman absolutely covered in smallpox; she was being led by a small child, presumably a grandchild. We felt so sorry for her as they were almost certain to perish on the way but there was literally nothing we could do.

That evening, the 18th, we arrived at a tiny village called Kunlong perched on the edge of a very steep ridge. It had been a hard climb up to this collection of huts, and on one of the last slopes we came across an Anglo-Indian gentleman who had been a lawyer in Toungoo when I had been stationed there in 1939-40. He was a very pleasant fellow, a member of the Club with his wife and two very charming daughters. He was now an officer in the Pay Corps and had collapsed on the side of the path. I stopped and spoke to him but he was past talking and it looked as if it was only a question of hours before he would die. Again we could do nothing, some of the party were already showing signs of real fatigue and even those of us who were fit had little reserve of strength. It was a sad ending to what had been a fairly reasonable day. About a year later I was amazed to meet this lawyer in India. He had, I gathered, spent the night where he lay and was able to carry on slowly the next day.

That night some of us slept in, some outside of, a tiny hut on the very edge of the ridge. Rain started during the night and it was bitterly cold with the wind whistling around this very exposed spot. The real bush Nagas always construct their villages on the tops of ridges to escape malaria. The valleys are usually very deep, narrow and well wooded, and are breeding grounds for the anopheles mosquito. The main disadvantage of these village sites is that water had to be obtained from streams 300 to 500 feet below by a path with a gradient of about one in two. It is an education to watch these Nagas walking; hills mean nothing to them and the women and even children walk up these awful slopes carrying two lengths of bamboo filled with water and arrive without any noticeable quickening of the breath. These water containers are usually pieces of hollow bamboo about three feet in length and about five inches in diameter inside. Some of the villagers were still in residence in this little hamlet and agreed to supply us with water at Rs.1/- (one shilling and sixpence) for each bamboo length, which contained possibly two quarts. We only wanted sufficient for tea and rice, all ideas of washing had to be abandoned at such a price.

It was still raining when we started off the next morning, the 19th. So far as I could gather we had kept up a fair average of about fifteen miles a day, possibly a little more on some days and we all looked that morning as if we were good for several more days in spite of being wet, shivering and miserable. We should need our strength as we were then at over 3,000 feet altitude and from the hills ahead of us we probably had another 2,000 feet to climb. The clouds were banking up everywhere and it was obvious that the rains had set in and we were in for several very unpleasant days.

It was a most miserable march that day with a bitter wind whistling across these very high hills. Clad in only a shirt and shorts and soaked to the skin one felt, and was, blue with cold. My wife was equally miserable as although she had an army oilskin mackintosh she had used it to wrap round her pack so as to keep her spare clothes dry. I had started off with a similar mackintosh but had given it to one of the men of the party who had a bad cough and looked as though he was on the verge of pneumonia.

We halted at a small village for our midday meal and in the afternoon had a long climb to the village of Koshen Kullen, which, according to the map we all studied when we got to India, is at an altitude of nearly 5,000 feet. Again we met a most helpful Headman who placed his house at our disposal, which was most welcome as we were all drenched through, the rain having been almost continuous. The house was a most amazing surprise, the walls and floor being made of two to three inch thick slabs of oak, each slab about four feet wide. The most comforting sight was a glowing fire of small logs.

The Nagas live by shifting cultivation. Every year during the cold weather a family will cut down an area of forest and after leaving this felled timber and bamboo to dry, will burn it just before the rains start. The bare burnt land is then sown up, the main crop being hill paddy. Next year a new area will be felled and so it goes on year after year, eventually all the natural forest being destroyed and areas will be cut over again and again on a rotation of about fifteen to twenty years according to the density of the population. During the whole of the march since crossing the Chindwin we had not seen a single tree more than about three feet in girth; these oak slabs must therefore have been hundreds of years old, obtained from the original virgin forest when the village was first formed. I longed for an elephant or two to enable me to purchase a few slabs and extract them to where I could get some really beautiful furniture made.

Neither my wife nor I are by any means slim though both of us lost a good deal of weight on that march, but we were both able to share one slab that night and share each other's blanket. We needed both blankets as in spite of the fire it was very cold. This fire was situated in the centre of the room on large stone slabs and was never allowed to go out. We piled it high with all the wood we could find in the hope that by next morning our clothes would be dry again.

This day's march had been our longest up till then, about seventeen miles, and had been a severe strain on several of the older members of the party. Three of them, for the first time since leaving Mansi, arrived after my wife, in spite of the fact that she had developed a very badly blistered heel and had limped the last few miles.

It was a wet and wild morning as we started off on the 20th, rather later than usual as we hated leaving the comfort of this house, it was so very unpleasant outside. However, we were going downhill, a good sign, with no large hills ahead of us. The path was very slippery and was alive with leeches. To anyone with no experience of the tropics that phrase 'alive with leeches' cannot convey a true picture. There were tens of thousands of these little brutes, all standing up on their tails wriggling about seeking for human flesh. Ever since the rains had started we had each night removed several of the little brutes

A Naga family

A Naga village

Left to right: Walter Voehringher, Andrewartha, author and wife, and Bob Forrest in Gulmerg (Kashmir), June, 1942

from around our ankles but on this day the socks of each one of us were very soon soaked in blood. At the end of each hour when we had our regular halt we all 'de-leeched' ourselves. No one dreamt of sitting down during those halts or at any other time though many did so involuntarily as in places it was almost impossible to keep upright it was so steep and slippery. Just before we arrived at our midday halt my wife had a very bad fall which for about five minutes completely winded her. Fortunately no permanent damage was done though she was covered in mud and for days afterwards one side was black and blue. We heard later that the Army had tried to send supplies by mule along this road but that two of the animals on the worst hill had fallen over the side and been lost.

At noon we arrived at Mollen where the Seaforth Highlanders had organised a food depot and where we were issued with flour, sugar, fat and tinned meat. We made an excellent breakfast, our faithful Sammy cooking chapattis which we had with the remains of the cold kid from the night before and also some tinned vegetables. Chapattis are flat pancake-like things and are wonderful when eaten piping hot. Our digestion was helped on by the good news that the path ran down to the plains, only a few miles ahead with a short way beyond that the Yarapok-Imphal motor road.

That last descent to the plains was extremely difficult, the slope was very steep and so slippery that one had to go sideways. Most of us, my wife included, several times lost our balance and found ourselves sliding down on our behinds. Quite a number of these falls were decidedly painful but with the thought that our march was nearly over we were ready to laugh at anything, and it was quite a hilarious party which slithered and slid down these last few remaining miles of hill country.

It was getting dusk when we arrived on the flat to be accosted by dozens of commercially-minded Manipuris selling the most revolting looking Indian made cigarettes for the most exorbitant price. We had not had a cigarette for days and days and even though their taste was as revolting as they looked we enjoyed those smokes. These cigarettes were called Rajah Shah and I think we paid one rupee per packet of ten. Later when we got to Calcutta we found they were the cheapest kind and should have been about twopence a packet.

The track seemed to go on for miles with both sides under cultivation, and the only village a mile or two off the road. It was almost dark, it was still raining and we were very wet and tired. We had done about twenty miles since Koshen Kullen, so decided to make for one of the villages off the track. What, however, looked like normal civilization turned out to be in places thick mud and marsh and that last hour or so floundering to the village seemed to be never ending. Our reception at the village was not by any means encouraging; all the Manipur inhabitants wanted was our money. After considerable argument they allowed us to sleep on the open mud floored verandah to the mosque, but on payment of Rs.50/-. These Manipuris are supposedly Brahmins, the highest caste of the Hindu religion, but I cannot believe they were typical of their caste.

Those villagers produced some jaggery, at a high price, also water, again at a high price; there was not one friendly gesture at any time and scores of them hovered round us for hours. At times they almost seemed menacing and we were very glad to get out of the place at the crack of dawn the next morning.

Those of us in our party who had been used to jungle life were very sorry to leave the hills; the views and scenery had been magnificent though none of us were in a fit state to admire and appreciate them. Had we had proper food and more time it would have been the most delightful trek. My wife and I both agreed that if we ever had a chance after the war we would take leave and with elephants and mules do the whole march again at our leisure. On the 21st we had about six miles to do to Yarapok where we found the Army had started up a canteen for Europeans and Anglos and we enjoyed an excellent breakfast of porridge, sausages, bacon and eggs. I was decidedly perturbed to find that no arrangements had been made for the Indian refugees, as we had seen so many cases of smallpox en route and had passed such dozens of corpses that it seemed madness to let this infected mob loose to roam at will through India to their homes.

I estimated we had covered about two hundred and forty miles on foot, taking fourteen and a half days, or roughly sixteen and a half miles per day. Once in the Naga Hills we had been obliged to go on until we reached a village and on one day covered twenty-three miles. But for the kindness and hospitality of the Naga villagers I think most of us would have gone down with pneumonia as almost every night we had arrived at a village drenched through, shivering with cold and often with our only spare clothes too wet to change into.

After breakfast we were fortunate in obtaining bullock carts to carry us to the main Tamu-Imphal road, a distance of about nine miles, and at the road junction our hearts were lightened by the sight of lorry after lorry passing. An Army ambulance stopped and gave about eight of us a lift into Imphal; after surviving the trek I was almost killed on that last journey. The ambulance driver went too close to a passing three-tonner which caught the back and ripped off the canvas cover and the iron supports. I was sitting with my feet over the back and one of the iron supports crashed down missing my head by less than an inch.

Still being concerned about the Indian refugees I asked to be taken to the Residency which we found had suffered in a bad bombing attack a day or two earlier. The Resident was using the remaining rooms which were intact. I then discovered that the message I had sent from Pyinbon had never been delivered. The messenger was the same officer who failed to return any of the 5,000 rupees I had given him when we left Mandalay; he was the only officer on my staff who let me down. Though several thousand refugees had already arrived the Resident had no inkling that there were at least twenty five thousand on the trek out. He could do nothing to help as the Army had taken over control and he directed me to Corps Headquarters. He also gave us a diagram showing the position of a camp for Europeans. A tea planter named Blenerhasset had been in control of this camp until a few days prior to our arrival at Imphal, but it had then been bombed by the Japanese when the senior lady helper had been killed with several of the occupants; it had since been abandoned. We now understood that a new camp had been formed and taken over by a senior Forest Officer from Burma who had been on the Tamu road organisation.

Returning to our ambulance we eventually found Corps Headquarters and after a short while I was able to repeat my story to a very charming and helpful Brigadier. He was horrified at the picture I presented but could do nothing as I had come to the wrong branch! The branch dealing with refugees was in another block of buildings about a mile away, so off we went again all feeling rather short tempered.

Arriving at the correct branch I was shown into a very large room occupied by two majors. For the third time I repeated my story, only this time standing up as these two little worms had not the manners to offer me a chair, though if I looked as I felt it must have been obvious that I was more than tired.

These two officers were about as useless as the Brigadier had been helpful; they appeared completely disinterested and bored and could only remark that as the Corps Commander was away nothing could be done till his return. As I left almost speechless with rage one did get up and ask me to point out on the map the position of the route we had taken. I met one of these officers about two years later at a dinner party in Delhi; I was not surprised to notice that he was still a major.

Returning to our ambulance we then searched for Blenerhasset's camp only to find on arriving there that it had been taken over a few days earlier by some military formation and used as a store. We were re-directed to a place a few miles out of Imphal down the Dimapur road.

Again we got into the ambulance, the driver of which was most patient and helpful, and eventually found the camp as it was called. It comprised a few scattered mud walled small houses and had once been a tiny village. The officer in charge had made himself comfortable in the largest hut even down to his camp bed and dressing table, his tin boxes and two cages containing his canaries which he had brought out of Burma. Except for some straw on the floor the other huts contained nothing. There were no latrines, and to wash one had to walk several hundred yards down to a stream the path being infected with leeches, and it was still pouring with rain and very cold. The drinking water came out from Imphal by motor transport and was therefore in limited supply.

Although we were Europeans, our reception by the Officer in charge of this camp could not have been colder until we met two human beings, one, the 'Orphan', whom I had last seen at Bamauk and the other, Atkinson, in the Indian Civil Service. They were grand and shepherded us all into a large room where we had an enormous meal. I was not feeling too grand as I had started what proved to be a go of dysentery and was also suffering from most painful piles.

It was pitch dark by then and we were only too ready for sleep, though rather disappointed at the lack of all amenities including lamps. We all made up our minds to get out of Imphal as soon as possible.

Before we got to bed the 'Orphan' and Atkinson wanted to hear all about our trek and immediately decided to collect all the medical supplies they could and go back down the road to see what help they could give. They left the next morning and on that very gallant errand of mercy Atkinson died of malaria.

We were all together again, the rest of my staff coming in on a lorry shortly after we had arrived.

Early on the 22nd we tried to find out how we could get transport to take us to Dimapur, the nearest railway station. The Officer in charge of the camp did nothing but we met a very pleasant Lieutenant-Colonel whom I had known in Burma, and at about 8 a.m. he arrived with the news that we could get lifts on a convoy leaving within an hour.

That was a hair-raising journey. My wife and I went in the leading fifteen hundredweight truck in which there were also an Indian doctor and his wife and four children. We also had our three dogs. The road to Dimapur through Kohima was still in course of construction; in parts it was just wide enough for a lorry with, on the inside, a sheer muddy wall rising for hundreds of feet and on the outside just space, with seemingly miles below the steamy jungle of a wooded valley. In places there had been a landslide and our lorry tilting at a frightening angle slithered in low gear across a sea of mud. At every bridge we could see below the remains of vehicles which had either crashed through the fragile wooden sides or had missed the bridge altogether and had slithered over the bank. There were three or four such wrecks down one stream.

At 2 p.m. we halted at Kohima for about three hours to let the 'up' traffic through as only one-way traffic was allowed on this road. I have often wondered why the Japanese did not bomb this road at this halting place; every day there must have been scores of lorries held up there presenting a magnificent target. The possibility of such an event was well in our minds as we halted there that day.

We heard later that one of the three-tonners behind us had been driven by an Indian with very inadequate training. At one of the landslides one of the rear wheels was over the edge and Condie, one of my officers who had been on our transport, took over and drove the vehicle the remaining seventy odd miles; this was although he had developed phlebitis on the march and both his legs were like balloons and agonizing.

We left at about 5 p.m. arriving at Dimapur four hours later. The seats in the truck had been getting harder and harder and ourselves more and more stiff and cramped. We halted a few miles outside Dimapur for a short while and it was then that our wire-haired terrier got up, gave herself a shake and dropped down dead. It was very sad as she had seemed so much better. My wife had been able to feed her on plenty of milk since reaching Imphal and we really thought she would survive the trip.

We made Dimapur just as dusk was falling and all entered an excellent camp set up solely for refugees. The longing and need for a hot bath was again frustrated as we found the only water in the wash place was stone cold. A good meal was provided and we were told that we could stay until a special refugee train was available. We did not like the sound of this, there were several hundreds in the camp and we might be stuck there for days. We still had some money left and all agreed to my suggestion that we should spend the night on the station and trust to luck to catch an ordinary train. It was wet and miserable hanging around on that bare platform, nothing can be more depressing than an Indian railway station, particularly a small up country one, but early in the morning a train appeared and we all managed to find some sort of accommodation. In our first-class compartment we had six Royal Air Force other ranks and about four of us plus dogs. The two upper berths for sleeping were put down and during the journey we took it in turns to sleep whilst the remainder were squashed in tight below. The Royal Air Force lads were full of cheer and for hours would roll out choruses at the top of their voices, at times in almost professional harmony.

We were still hungry and the sight of the itinerant Indian food-stuff vendors at each station was too tempting. Where and how the messes had been cooked it was advisable not to enquire, but they looked good and we ate them. They tasted good, too, though if any of us had not got dysentery then we certainly deserved to get it. The Royal Air Force lads were very young and seemed to have larger appetites even than ours. Fortunately in addition to the Indian food-stuff vendors the Assam Tea Planters Association had at all the main stations provided canteens which were run by the Planter's wives who were wonderfully good.

At the Brahmaputra river we had to embark on the river ferry where a really excellent meal which I had ordered by telegram was awaiting us. I think we all enjoyed sitting at tables with spotless napery and being able to order a whiskey and soda even more than the excellent food provided.

On the other side we again came up against the desire of every official to send us on by refugee train. Admittedly we were filthy dirty, we had not had a bath since the 18th and it was now the 24th and our clothes were in a shocking state. I had had my topee stolen, my wife's topee had collapsed in the rain and we were both wearing enormous wide brimmed Chin bamboo hats. Possibly the powers that be quite rightly thought we would contaminate any ordinary first-class carriage.

However, after snooping around we discovered a train waiting at one of the platforms; it was completely empty, so we spread ourselves out and got down to a much-needed sleep. It was then about 10 p.m. Just as we were dozing off, the Railway Transport Officer turned up and wanted us to get out as

CHAPTER XIII

During the next few weeks we were able to collect the stories from members of the staff who had been in different parties on the various routes out.

Lusk turned up in Calcutta a few days after our arrival and we then heard of the tragic, but gallant death of Pughe. Their party instead, as we hoped, of being able to raft down the river from Kyauksegyi to Tonhe, had been obliged on the third day with the falling of the river to take to the path. Their rafts repeatedly stuck in sandbanks or in shallows. By the second night they were utterly exhausted with pushing and dragging these unwieldy bamboo structures into deep water channels only to go aground again a few minutes later.

It was a very anxious time for Lusk as so many of his party were elderly and unaccustomed to trekking. Pughe soon became a casualty as his leg could not stand up to the very rough walking, and they were obliged to make a rough stretcher on which he was carried by Indian labourers. They eventually got to Tonhe in the evening three days after we did, only to be turned out of the town by the Chinese as the Japanese had been reported a few miles down the river. The party went on for about a mile or so and camped for the night beside the path. Early the next morning they were woken by the noise of the Japanese attacking Tonhe, trench mortar and rifle fire being incessant. This was too much for the Indians in Lusk's party all but one of whom disappeared.

Lusk got the party moving and he and one other member with Pughe's faithful Indian servant tried to persuade Pughe to tackle the march with their support. This very gallant gentleman refused to be a hindrance and insisted on being left behind. Knowing the path I don't think Lusk and the others would ever have been able to get Pughe out; in many places the path wound its way round the side of steep hills where it would have been impossible to use a stretcher, whilst along other portions the slopes were too steep for any one man to carry another. However, Lusk and the others spent some time trying to persuade Pughe to make the effort. Like Captain Oates on Scott's Antarctic Expedition of 1910 Pughe elected to risk almost certain death rather than be a burden on his comrades. It was a ghastly experience for Lusk, and when he told me the story I could see how bitter was the memory of being forced to leave the man lying there helpless.

From subsequent stories we heard that the Chinese rearguard found Pughe and gave him a lift on their ponies, but even that effort was too much for him, he fell off and was left at the side of the path. Later an Indian refugee reported that he saw Pughe shot by the Japanese as he staggered off the path to hide in the surrounding jungle. One can only be grateful that this gallant Englishman died suddenly rather than having to endure days of agony of starvation and thirst.

The rest of the party made Imphal, but two, I think, subsequently died there, neither of them members of my staff.

Ricketts, after I left him at Mohnyin on 3rd May spent a hectic twenty-four hours acquiring premises for use as a camp, and on the 4th was in the process of accommodating one thousand evacuees who had arrived by train when he received a message from me, sent from Naba, telling him to start for India at once. The next morning he met at Hopin the acting Home Secretary who had come down from

Myitkyina, and learned that the arrival of the Japanese was only a question of a few hours. He also received instructions to conduct as many refugees as he could out to India via the Hopin-Tamanthelayshi-Somra-Manipur route.

Ricketts then explained the situation to the evacuees but the vast majority refused to leave, being convinced the train would go on to Myitkyina. Early on the 6th, therefore, he collected those who were prepared to join him, ninety-two all told of whom only seven were Europeans, and started off. Of these Europeans three were Army non-commissioned officers, one was a seaman from the Burma Navy and one was another member of my staff.

From 6th May to the 14th they covered nearly eighty miles with the help of at first carts and then elephants. On the night of the 14th all the elephant attendants disappeared and the party was increased by the arrival of seventeen more refugees amongst whom were two privates of the King's Own Yorkshire Light Infantry. From then on until 21st June they covered a further hundred and ninety miles, arriving on that day at Phikrokedzuma where there was a hospital and where a refugee organisation working from Assam had supplies of all refugees' needs. They had often only been able to cover a few miles a day owing to the presence of five infants and thirty-four children in the party. Malaria and dysentery attacked almost every member of the party, and at one time out of forty-five coolies they obtained from villages thirty-nine were used to carry the sick. For days they had been held up by flooded streams which were impossible to cross. Of the original party nine died and there were other casualties amongst those who joined them during the march. Ricketts and the other member of my staff were both admitted to hospital with dysentery on the 21st, and could not carry out the last stage of their journey till the 28th when they arrived at Kohima. Like Lusk's party on one occasion during the march they had escaped the Japanese by only twelve hours.

The alternative route from Myitkyina was via the Hukong valley, which, as I have mentioned in an earlier chapter, was almost impassable once the rains broke. Twenty to thirty thousand must have attempted to get to India via this route and, although no reliable figures are available, deaths must have been not less than fifteen to twenty per cent. Conditions were ghastly, the mud was more than knee deep, the rain was often continuous, leeches and mosquitoes were in their millions, streams were flooded and unfordable and mile after mile the dead and dying lined the path.

Figures are available of the number of refugees who arrived in India by air, sea and on foot and all told it is estimated that four hundred thousand were safely evacuated. Counting the cholera epidemics of the Taungup Pass and at Mandalay and the thousands who died on the march out, I have estimated that the total casualties were about fifteen thousand – a ghastly figure when considered by itself, but a little less terrible when considered with the number who gained safety in India.

Not a few of that large number succumbed later to the privation and hardship they had endured or to the after-effects of malaria and dysentery. Of my staff Booth Russell and Bob Forrest both died within twelve months at a Calcutta hospital, Ricketts had to leave the service on account of lung trouble and Bott died in Assam. By now others too may have passed on.

Some of those who remained behind were fortunate, others very much less so. Amongst the fortunate were the Hamiltons. They got to Myitkyina, passengers taking turns to drive the engine after the driver and stoker had run away. They then moved out some miles to a Gurkha village and there they spent the years until Myitkyina was retaken by the American and Chinese. They were occasionally visited by Japanese troops but were never molested. Others who remained in the town were confined to special camps by the Japanese and many were killed during the recapture of the town when they attempted to escape to the Chinese and American lines. In the half-light of dawn the Chinese thought it was an attack and opened fire.

Most of those left at Naba sought sanctuary in the surrounding villages and for some time were left undisturbed. Later many were moved to the south by the Japanese whilst others were made to work as servants to the Burmese who, with the arrival in the District of Aung San's rebel army, were forced or persuaded to become somewhat anti-British.

Looking back on it all now, after nine years, one asks oneself was it all a ghastly tragedy, a miserable failure, and could the chaos and confusion have been avoided? I don't think any definite answer to those questions is possible. The cancellation of the original Evacuation scheme was undoubtedly a mistake as had it remained in force only essential workers would have remained in Rangoon. Whether Government would have been strong enough to insist on the evacuation of all non-essential women and children is a matter of considerable doubt, as is also the question of whether the large female and child Anglo-Indian and Anglo-Burman population would have left their husbands and fathers. A large proportion of this class had no savings and required every anna of their pay to exist even when living together. It is doubtful if they could have afforded to maintain two separate establishments.

However, the original evacuation scheme was mainly for the benefit of the non-indigenous population, who were principally Indians, and the Burmese Ministers were not prepared to incur the very heavy expenditure the scheme envisaged mainly for the benefit of such people. The air evacuation from Myitkyina was undoubtedly an avoidable failure, the responsibility for which has yet to be made public. Even if India was not to blame, that vast country never appreciated the difficulties we were up against and its Government, even after we arrived in India, did very little to ease the plight of the Burma refugee. The majority of the assistance was given by private civilian organisations, the Assam Tea Planter's Association, with their orderly and well-stocked camps on the more northerly evacuation routes, being responsible for saving hundreds of lives.

The tragedies on the various land routes taken by refugees would, with such short notice, have been almost impossible to avoid. On the other hand the Hukong Valley route would never have been used had air evacuation been efficient. The same might have applied to the route we followed through Tonhe, as all the refugees at Katha and Naba could have gone north and been flown out in less than a week if the planes eventually requisitioned at Dingyan aerodrome had been available two or three weeks earlier.

The Tamu-Imphal route, finally made motorable by the Army and used so extensively during the re-occupation of Burma in 1944-45, had been under discussion as a major work in the Government's road programme for at least the past twenty years. There was at one time a proposal to extend the Mandalay-Monywa railway to India and I believe I am correct in stating that years earlier an alignment had actually been completed. Why the projects were dropped only those in very high places can explain, but amongst the ordinary public the general impression had always been that the vested shipping interests used their enormous influence, and had a very large say in preventing such construction which undoubtedly would have had an adverse effect on their traffic receipts.

The Taungup tragedy could have only been prevented by Dictatorship methods. No one could have envisaged such mass, suicidal migration and, as I have mentioned in an earlier chapter, it would have taken months, if not a year or more, to render this route fit for evacuation. Nothing would have stopped that exodus in December 1941 and in early 1942 except possibly machine guns, and even had that mass been stopped, without adequate shipping to evacuate them from Rangoon it might have only delayed the tragedy.

There was never sufficient sea transport but I doubt if that was anybody's fault. With the far greater needs of the war in the west the ships were not available. The whole Empire could not be kept intact, something had to be sacrificed if we were to survive in Europe. I always remember a conference in London in 1944 when I was endeavouring to obtain civil supplies for the re-occupation of Burma. After several hours of discussion with officials from every military and civil Department concerned, the conference came to an abrupt conclusion with a remark made by a high-ranking War Office official to the effect that though they all appreciated our needs they were not interested in the East, all their efforts were concentrated on the war in Europe. That attitude had been forced on those in authority ever since 1940.

However, in spite of the tragedies, the chaos and confusion, all in Burma in those days did, I think, succeed in doing their job. That very gallant Army of ours, so hopelessly outnumbered, held back the Japanese till the rains broke and thus prevented an immediate march on India, an attack which India was certainly not then in a position to withstand.

The civil officials carried on at their posts till more often than not the Japanese were almost at their gates. The British official out East has often been accused of egotistical bigotry and obstinacy but during those days in Burma there were very few who failed to react to the ever-changing conditions and who did not place their duty and affection for the people before all considerations of their own personal safety.

What about the people themselves? Many who did not really know the Burmese considered them during 1941-45 the worst type of traitor and enemy, yet during the six months covered by this book and during the military administration in 1945 not one single Government official was killed or wounded by the Burmese and not one European civilian was attacked or molested during the evacuation. On the contrary, all of whom I have met received from the Burmese villagers every possible assistance and respect and, when we returned in 1945, both officials and non-officials received a warm welcome in every part of the country.

There was a bad element as there is in any group of human beings; and this is not helped by a rather different attitude to life and death. Considering how these people had been taught for years to rely and depend on us it is, I think, very surprising that their loyalty stood up to the shock of seeing all they trusted and believed in collapsing in a few short months.

In the whole Burma campaign there was no lack of publicity of the unpleasant incidents, but there was seldom any reference to the magnificent support and loyalty we received from most of the Burmese and from the Karens, the Chins, Kachins and Nagas. Many of the latter did not want independence in 1947; they still remembered and had faith in the integrity and individuality of the British District Administrator but this loyalty and faith received a mortal blow when independence was granted to Burma before, they felt, their own political needs had been understood or protected within the country's new Constitution.

So far as the Evacuation Department was concerned I don't think it was possible to have done more. Conditions were so abnormal, nothing was simple, nothing was definite, nothing was static. There were never periods of calm in which to recover from the chaotic disturbances of the periods of confusion. Decisions and plans made one day had to be completely changed a day or two after, servants would disappear without warning, food supplies, water, all the necessities of life available one day were scarce or completely absent the next. Added to all that was my constant need for reliable staff which I had to trust to luck to collect from anywhere and everywhere. Up till 14th April one, and only one, officer was officially posted to me by Government, and never during the whole six months did Government acknowledge the need for staff by sanctioning rates of pay. We were always a Cinderella Department, which, however, had its advantages; it gave me unlimited authority, and being practically independent of Government we were dependent on each other which created a feeling of camaraderie and an esprit de corps which enabled us to work together as a happy family. None of them, except Ricketts and me, had any future to look forward to in Government service; each and every one of them was out to do the best they could. In all that very mixed staff who stayed on till the end there is only one whom I can remember shirking, grousing or at any time letting me down. No one could have wished for a more loyal and splendid staff.

No book on the evacuation would be complete without a word of admiration for the courage and patient endurance of the refugees themselves. Most of them were uneducated peasants who, though accustomed to rough conditions and hardships, were totally inexperienced in the horrors of war, utterly ignorant of the terror of high explosive and incendiary bombs. Others were town bred people who probably never in their lives had slept out of a bed in a well built house and had never dreamt of walking more than a few miles round a golf course. Many of them were of poor physique and almost all of them were burdened with the care of little children. Yet with infinite patience and fortitude they put up with the hardships of camp life, the fear of frequent bombing or of death from cholera and smallpox which was all around them. They then tackled without flinching the uncertainties and perils of a march of hundreds of miles through unknown, often uninhabited and always malarial jungle. The difficulties of the Manipur route or even the Taungup route were as nothing compared to the later stages of the evacuation over the Naga Hills and the Hukong valley. When all the stories of these journeys come to be written by those who have personal knowledge of them there will surely be many a tale of courage, kindness and self-sacrifice. Yet even in what we saw with our own eyes there was much to bring a catch to the breath or a tear to the eye.

There is an old book, beloved of childhood days, John Bunyan's *Pilgrims' Progress*. All the characters were to be met on our journey. Mr. Worldly Wiseman was there, Money-love, Timorous, Ignorance and even Mr. Malice. But more often we came across Mr. Hopeful, Mr. Valiant for Truth, Mr. Steadfast and Mr. Greatheart. Christian and Christiana his wife were there too, with Mercy and Prudence. Many like the soldiers who fought so valiantly and so well to give us time, laid down their lives; Mrs. Munroe killed in the raid at Pyinmana, Mr. Williams who died of cholera, Major Pughe, ill and weak, refusing to take the easy way out, and having to be left, many more who helped others through, only to succumb at the end to exhaustion and fever. Some of their names we know, others not yet, many we shall never know.

Let us borrow a phrase from Bunyan:

"So they passed over and all the trumpets sounded for them on the other side."

APPENDIX I

DIARY OF ESCAPE, 2nd - 25th May 1942

Daily Schedule:
Rise at dawn, have small meal and walk till 11 a.m.; rest until 3 p.m., have cup of tea and walk till dusk when evening meal eaten; also a brief rest halt made every hour; five grains quinine taken daily.

2nd May
Katha to Indaw
My wife with some staff by car.

3rd May
Indaw to Pyinbon
By car staying at Forest Department bungalow.

4th May
At Pyinbon
Three remaining evacuation staff girls arrived plus McLean and McAughtrie to take control of group.

5th May
Pyinbon to Mansi
My wife and party walked fourteen miles except older members given help with jeep as ferry.

6th May
Mansi to Magyigon by noon and on for night to sandbank in middle of Chaunggyi river bed
I arrived in early hours and all left on foot at dawn. Jeep ferrying the unfit and elderly jeep abandoned.

7th May
Continued to Kyauksegyi
Waited for rest of staff who arrived in afternoon.

8th May
Left 3 p.m with night on Chaunggyi river bank
Group now fifty so divided into two of 25 with raft being made for less fit group. Joined by some Indian refugees paid to help with loads.

APPENDIX II

INDEX OF PERSONALITIES

ACKNOWLEDGEMENTS

I have to thank Sir Robert Hutchings, K.C.I.E., C.M.G., for kindly allowing me to use extracts from his official report on the Evacuation of Burma.

The painting on the dust jacket of a part of Mandalay is by R.Talbot Kelly and is taken from his book *Burma*, first published in 1905 by Adam and Charles Black.

The map of Rangoon's environs is from a pamphlet by Mr. T.L. Hughes published by Brittain Publishing Company.

The photographs on pages 21 (IND 808), 55 and 56 (IND 861 & 865) are courtesy of the Imperial War Museum.

The photographs on pages 8, 14, 25, and 114 are courtesy of George Rodger/TimePix.

The photograph on page 40 (10R MSS EUR) is by permission of the British Library.